A
PLACE OF
HEALING

A PLACE OF HEALING

WRESTLING *with the* MYSTERIES *of* SUFFERING, PAIN, *and* GOD'S SOVEREIGNTY

JONI EARECKSON TADA

David C Cook®
transforming lives together

CADCC

A PLACE OF HEALING
Published by David C. Cook
4050 Lee Vance View
Colorado Springs, CO 80918 U.S.A.

David C. Cook Distribution Canada
55 Woodslee Avenue, Paris, Ontario, Canada N3L 3E5

David C. Cook U.K., Kingsway Communications
Eastbourne, East Sussex BN23 6NT, England

David C. Cook and the graphic circle C logo
are registered trademarks of Cook Communications Ministries.

All rights reserved. Except for brief excerpts for review purposes,
no part of this book may be reproduced or used in any form
without written permission from the publisher.

The Web site addresses recommended throughout this book are offered as a
resource to you. These Web sites are not intended in any way to be or imply an
endorsement on the part of David C. Cook, nor do we vouch for their content.

LCCN 2010928036
ISBN 978-1-4347-6532-1
eISBN 978-0-7814-0505-8
International Trade Paperback ISBN 9781434702067

The Team: Don Pape, Susan Tjaden, Amy Kiechlin, Sarah Schultz, Erin Prater, Karen Athen
Designer: JWH Graphic Arts, James Hall
Image: Getty Images, dellafels. Rights managed.

Printed in the United States of America
First Edition 2010

2 3 4 5 6 7 8 9 10

012811

For

Gracie Rosenberger
and
Barbara Coleman

Two of my special "pain pals."
Every day these women live where
our worst fears threaten to take us;
yet they do so with consummate trust in God
and graciousness toward family and friends.

Thank you, Gracie and Barbara, for
inspiring me to do the same.

CONTENTS

Thankful for These ...

Healing and help. Those two words go together so well. When someone struggles with pain, a helping hand is so appreciated. And I'm no exception. Especially as I worked on *A Place of Healing,* for the subtitle says it all: *Wrestling with the Mysteries of Suffering, Pain, and God's Sovereignty.* There were days of such physical pain that I had to wrestle to write even one page. But God graciously sent some incredibly helpful people my way.

Like Larry Libby. I have worked with my trusty editor-friend on previous books, but never have I had to lean on him as hard as with *A Place of Healing.* Larry was able to hold a "stethoscope" up to my soul and give language to the stirrings and murmurs inside my heart—for that, I am eternally grateful. If anyone walks away from this book having drawn closer to God and His Word, I have you to thank, Larry.

And I'm always leaning on Wolgemuth & Associates for help. Robert and Bobbie Wolgemuth are longtime friends with whom I have harmonized on many a hymn, not to mention collaboration on past books. They are also intimately acquainted with the path of pain I've journeyed on these many years, and so I thank you for your prayers, Robert and Bobbie. I'm indebted to the growing team at Wolgemuth & Associates, especially Erik and Andrew—God bless you both for opening doors for me to wheel through.

11

The good folks at David C. Cook have helped give a big boost to *A Place of Healing*. From Dan Rich to Don Pape: *Thank you* for extending the Cook platform to me so that I can share my story with a new generation of readers. I'm especially grateful to Erin Prater and Susan Tjaden, who became real cheerleaders for the book, giving care and thought in refining every page and paragraph.

There were plenty of times at Joni and Friends when I had to pull away from the computer and simply lie down to give my body a break. It takes a team of people to not only help me research and type, but to get me sitting up comfortably in my wheelchair and moving forward. My coworkers—Judy Butler, Francie Lorey, Rainey Floreen, Amy Donahue, and Jaime Chambers—deserve a round of applause for the many times they lent a hand.

Finally, special thanks to my dear husband, Ken, who has faithfully walked beside my chair these many years, seeing me through every hurt and happiness. Ken and I pray that the insights I've shared in *A Place of Healing* will lift the spirits of the reader to new heights of trust and confidence in our wonderfully sovereign God—He is our very present *help* for every need; He is our place of healing.

FOREWORD

I have always had the deepest respect for Joni Eareckson Tada even though I have never met her in person. I have heard her talk, listened to her on the radio, purchased her artwork—actually it was my wife—and read her books. She has lived with a disability for over forty years and has done it with faith and hope. She is one remarkable person! Ten years ago I went from respecting her to becoming a fellow pilgrim with her. Ten years ago I was diagnosed with ALS—also known as Lou Gehrig's disease. It is an incurable and fatal disease. The doctors gave me two to five years to live and most of that would be in a disabled condition. The disease robs the nerves of their ability to work and so the muscles quit working. The future is about wheelchairs, feeding tubes, and breathing assistance. Like Joni, I have outlived the doctor's predictions. So I was excited to read *A Place of Healing*.

I could not put this book down. The questions Joni asks and the struggles she shares were as if she was reading my mind. I have the same questions and struggles. I cried as I read, and occasionally I laughed. It was as if she was writing for me. I like the fact that Joni is writing in the midst of her terrible pain. I am generally not happy with people who have never walked "through the valley of the shadow of death." I want to hear from people who are currently walking through that valley. They offer me more encouragement and hope. And this book is filled with encouragement and hope.

Joni is honest about her pain. Even though I do not have pain with my disease, I felt she was talking to me—heart to heart and soul to soul. She is honest about the subject of healing. I have never known anyone who has been healed of ALS. I know God is capable—just as He is capable of healing Joni. But most of all she is honest about how you deal with pain, struggles, and suffering. She tells stories from her own life and the lives of others, and fills the book with quotations from the Bible (this is the best part of the book). This is a must-read for anyone who, like me, struggles each day and those who help and care for those who struggle. I can summarize the book in one word: *brilliant.* Or maybe *encouraging.* Or maybe *biblical.* Or maybe *honest.* Okay—it cannot be summed up in one word. It is the story of one person dealing with pain and struggles who, in the telling it, offers hope to to the rest of us who struggle.

Ed Dobson,

author of *The Year of Living Like Jesus* and *Prayers and Promises When Facing a Life-Threatening Illness*

INTRODUCTION

The fact of suffering undoubtedly constitutes
the single greatest challenge to the Christian
faith, and has been in every generation.
—John Stott

It was a beautiful Sunday morning, and services were over. I was wheeling across the church parking lot toward my van when a handsome young man, who introduced himself as David, stopped me.

"Are you Joni?" he asked.

I smiled, nodding yes.

"Oh great!" David exclaimed. "I'm a visitor here, and I was hoping I would run into you today. I've really been praying for you."

My eyes got wide. "Really? What about?"

"Your healing. I've been praying for you to get out of your wheelchair."

At that point, my spirit hesitated. David was a visitor. He came to church hoping to see me, and he wanted to see me healed. I can't tell you how many people I've met over the years who've done the same thing. In churches, on street corners, in convention centers, and in busy shopping malls. Some of those encounters have been a little overwhelming—almost frightening.

But not on this day, with this young man.

Still, I had to fight off eerie feelings. Several times, years ago, a group of men showed up at our farmhouse door in Maryland, all having been led there by the Holy Spirit to either heal me … or marry me! So perhaps you can understand my reticence.

"Well, I never refuse a prayer for healing," I assured David.

This guy wasted no time in getting down to business, launching into what sounded like a prepared speech. "Have you ever considered that it might be sin standing in the way of your healing? That you've disobeyed in some way?" Before I could answer, David flipped open his Bible—both of us still in the middle of the parking lot—and read from the gospel of Luke, "Some men came carrying a paralytic on a mat and tried to take him into the house to lay him before Jesus. When they could not find a way to do this because of the crowd, they went up on the roof and lowered him on his mat through the tiles into the middle of the crowd, right in front of Jesus" (5:18–19).

He closed his Bible and reminded me that the paralyzed man in the story was healed. And I could be, too, if only I would but confess my sins and have faith to believe. He added, "Joni, there *must* be some sin in your life that you haven't dealt with yet."

I told him that my conscience was clean before the Lord (he looked a little skeptical about that) and reiterated that I always welcome prayers for healing. I thanked him for his concern but told him I didn't think this was a matter of faith.

For David, that just didn't add up. According to what he had been taught, if I was a Christian, and if there was no known sin in my life, and if I had faith that God could heal, well, then … *I would be healed.* Didn't God want everyone healed? Didn't Jesus want everyone well? Of course He did! It was so obvious!

"Joni, you must have a lack of faith. I mean, look at you. You're still in your wheelchair!"

I thought for a moment about the biblical account he had just read me and asked him to open up his Bible again to that same passage,

Luke 5. "Okay," I said, "you're right about one thing, David. Right after they lowered the paralyzed man through the roof and to the floor in front of Jesus, he was healed. But look at verse 20. It says that when Jesus *saw the faith of those four friends*, the man was made well."

"So?"

"Don't you see? He didn't require anything at all of the disabled man. What He was looking for was faith in those men who had lowered him through the roof. God doesn't require *my* faith for healing. But He could require *yours*. The pressure's off me, David. If God has it in His plan to lift me out of this wheelchair, He could use *your* faith! So keep believing, friend; the pressure's on *you!*"

David didn't like that point of view. Again, it wasn't according to his script. It wasn't what he had been taught. According to all his teachers, if a person wasn't healed, it had to be a problem with *him*, with *his* faith.

Faith, however, is not the focus.

The focus is always on Jesus Christ and His will for those who suffer. To possess great faith is to believe in a great Savior, and Scripture welcomes the faith of *anyone* who believes in Jesus' will to heal. In the days to come, that "anyone" could well be David.

Do we even need to say it?

God certainly does heal today, and there's no doubt about it. To render any other verdict would be to ignore both the clear witness of God's Word and the heartfelt testimonies of many grateful and exultant brothers and sisters around the world who want nothing more than to bring glory to the name of their Savior and Healer.

But reflecting on my recent parking–lot experience with David, perhaps that very statement—"God heals today"—requires closer scrutiny.

Does He *always* heal? Does He heal *everyone* who comes to Him in faith? Does He miraculously intervene in the lives of *all* who pray for release from migraine headaches ... multiple sclerosis ... prostate cancer ... a bad case of the flu ... or, in my case, chronic pain?

And if not, then why not? And why does He heal some and not others?

Notice I didn't even bring up quadriplegia with spinal cord injury in this context. Those long-ago and faraway days of pleading with God to raise me up on my feet and out of my wheelchair are behind me. Oh, I'm still in my wheelchair. But I'm happy. And on *that* level, I have been healed. Big time.

Right now the big question for me is all about pain. (Yes, I know you're probably wondering how it is that a completely paralyzed person can *feel* pain at all. Trust me. At *my* age at least, one can.) Frankly, if this pain weren't so chronic, so jaw splitting at times, I'd leave it alone. But just as I used to tell Him years ago when I was first injured, I find myself once again praying, *Lord, I can't live like this for the rest of my life!*

At least I don't think I can. That remains to be seen.

Now don't get me wrong. I'm not "taking back" anything I've written about miraculous healing in articles or even in my 1978 book, *A Step Further.* (Could that really have been over thirty years ago?) But this ongoing urgency has forced me to look back on familiar Scriptures and give them another turn or two, examining them a little more closely from new angles—and from a different perspective.

My friends, this is new turf for me.

As Joshua once told the children of Israel, "You have never been this way before." And so it is with me. I have never been in such a place in all my life. But just as the Israelites found the Lord on both sides (and in the middle) of the Jordan, so I am finding His presence, His comfort, and His faithfulness in this strange and alien country of increased suffering.

This book isn't meant to be a detailed and exhaustive theological review of every verse in the Bible that seems to allude to miraculous healing. Much of why God does what He does and heals when He heals remains cloaked in divine mystery, and I certainly won't be the one unwrapping those things in these few pages. Instead, I will be inviting you to join me on a contemporary and very personal journey as I return to some foundational questions about life and healing, suffering and perseverance, heartbreak and hope.

I also want to encourage us to look up from day-to-day battles to focus on that time of ultimate healing awaiting us all. The time when every eye will be opened, the ears of all those who are deaf will be unstopped, the tongues of those who cannot speak will shout for joy, and the lame shall leap like deer (Isaiah 35). Oh what a glorious day that will be!

For those of us who do *not* experience a miracle of physical healing in our present earthly lives, can we hang on? Can we hold onto hope? And more than just holding on, can we learn what we *should* learn during our "period of captivity"? (That's what it feels like on days when my pain nearly drives me crazy.)

Do I pray for miraculous healing for my chronic pain? *You bet I do.*

Am I expecting it? *If God wills, yes.*

"Whatever You want, Lord," I pray. "If it would give You more glory and advance Your gospel more quickly, I'm all for it!" Always and always I want to be in submission to the Father and obedient to the Word of Jesus—knowing full well that if I had everything else in life and lacked *that*, I would have nothing at all.

Because isn't that the bottom line? That Jesus gets the glory, whether I jump out of my wheelchair pain free and tell people that my healing is genuine evidence of God's awesome power ... or whether I continue smiling in my chair, not in spite of my pain but because of it, knowing I've got lessons to learn, a character to be honed, other wounded people to identify with, a hurting world to reach with the gospel, and a suffering Savior with whom I can enjoy greater intimacy. And every bit of it genuine evidence of God's love and grace.

The book you hold in your hands is a chronicle of what I am going through right now. For the past five years I've been in the wrestling ring with an enemy that seems to grow larger, more fiendish and hatefully aggressive, with each passing month. I am speaking of my ongoing battle with pain—sometimes slow and grinding, sometimes white-hot and seemingly unbearable. In fact, as I write these words, I am seeing yet another specialist to see if there is anything—anything at all—that can be done for a simmering agony I would gladly and with great joy and gratitude leave behind.

I wanted to weave *that* aspect of my life into these pages as well. Not for sensational purposes, but simply because that is where I am and who I am. As you will see, writing a book about God's healing from a platform of intense suffering gives an urgency to the subject that keeps it from becoming detached or academic.

Healing—or even a brief respite from the pain war—is certainly uppermost in my mind these days.

No ... let me amend that. Bringing honor to the name of my Savior and King is uppermost, whether He chooses to give me relief now or just around the corner in His Father's house. Either way, He will help me and save me and, yes, crown me with joy.

Just as He always has.

ONE

REPORT FROM THE FRONT LINES

If God sends us on strong paths, we
are provided strong shoes.

—Corrie ten Boom

This is no time to write a book.

But I have to try.

It won't be easy. It may not be wise. Nevertheless, if you are reading these words, it has been accomplished, and the book has been published. God be thanked!

So mark it here. I am taking on a task that in-the-know book writers wouldn't attempt, and setting myself to complete an assignment that military historians would never dream of undertaking. I am writing in the midst of my experience, in the violence of a firefight, in the crush of circumstances, and in the vice grip of unrelenting pain. I am recording my combat-zone observations before the smoke has cleared, before the shells have stopped falling, before the guns have gone silent, before the long grass and wildflowers have grown over the scars of war.

And I am writing with great urgency. My life is changing, and I want to speak to these issues of suffering in a believer's life—and yes, to God's undeniable healing power—while I still can. Incessant pain, as those who have lived in its grip can attest, makes it very difficult to think, work, relate, plan, write, and—as I recently discovered—take on a public-speaking opportunity.

Not long ago I was invited to speak to a class at Biola University here in Los Angeles, California. I'd been asked to address Dr. Kathy McReynolds's class on "A Theology of Suffering and Disability," a course designed by Biola and our Christian Institute on Disability here at the Joni and Friends International Disability Center. Dr. McReynolds had asked me to come and lecture her sixty-five students on how God redeems suffering. And some of those students, she had told me, had deeper questions than that.

The class met in one of those classrooms in the older part of campus that has no windows—and precious little ventilation. The professor had placed a fan near one of the doors, which I appreciated. Still, without windows and on a warm day in Southern California, the room immediately seemed hot and close.

Before I could even be introduced, I felt those familiar sensations of the walls closing in on me.

Claustrophobia, my old nemesis.

It was the same feeling that comes when I wake up at 2 a.m., after the pain medication has worn off and Ken is sleeping soundly. In those dark, middle-of-the-night moments, I'm not physically able to free myself from a too-hot blanket, and the stiffness of lying in one position for so many hours overtakes me with a rush of pain that dares me to try to fall asleep again.

Dr. McReynolds introduced me to the class, and I looked across the room as I began. Some young, fresh-faced juniors leaned forward on their elbows, anticipating, I gathered, something bright and inspirational. Others slouched, fiddling with their pencils. Those were probably the ones with the "deeper questions." *Well, welcome to the club.*

I began where I have begun a thousand times before: with my own testimony. The hot summer morning at Chesapeake Bay. The raft, the dive, the impact, the injury, the Stryker frame in a Baltimore hospital … the long years of treatment and therapy, and the beginnings of an unimaginable ministry. From there I bridged into the whole question of God's will. *How could God allow all this to happen in my life?* Although I try to make it fresh, I have to admit there are times when it all sounds a little too rote, a little too pat in my own ears.

But not this time.

Fresh Urgency

At this stage of my life the question bears down on me with fresh urgency, just as it did in that very moment in the classroom. Although I'd tried hard to get my corset right before the class, and although I'd been lifted up, carefully positioned, and repositioned repeatedly that day, I was hurting.

I mean *really* hurting.

Fifteen minutes into my talk I found myself squirming in my wheelchair and biting my lip, struggling to express even familiar thoughts and ideas. And the room was *so* warm. It felt like an extra effort just getting my breath.

I somehow muddled through my allotted forty-five minutes. But it had felt like a muddle. Had the students gained anything from it? Their faces told me at least some had been moved—perhaps even deeply. Certainly no one was slouching or doodling now. Had God done something mysterious with my labored presentation—something beyond what I could have reasonably expected? (How many times He has done that before!)

After a short break it was time for the question-and-answer segment. Most of the questions were pretty predictable, but for whatever reason, one of those common, expected questions suddenly pierced deeply, touching some nerve I hadn't even realized was raw.

"You mentioned that you're going through a season of pain," the student began. "I would think it would be awfully distracting from your main mission. Why do you think God allowed this?"

Why, indeed.

Why has *God allowed this? I'm almost sixty years old! Why such agony and distraction at this point in my journey, after all these years of enduring, persevering, and seeking to serve Him?*

The simple question, like driftwood hidden in heavy surf, came at me in a wave of fresh pain. It's not like I hadn't dealt with that issue a million times. I've handled that "why does God allow this" query on countless occasions in numberless settings in multiple languages throughout the course of my paralyzed life, but … for some reason, I found it terribly difficult to answer in that moment. *Was it because I was tired? Lack of sleep will do that to you. Was it because the room was stuffy and the fan wasn't working? Was it because I'd stopped quietly pleading with God for His mercy?*

My throat thickened and my eyes welled with tears. I started to answer. I had the words on my tongue. But I had to stop. I took short breaths to gain composure, but my nose began to run and tears escaped my lower lids.

Yeah, I'd lost it, and the students all knew it.

Now what?

I didn't want to make a scene. Didn't want the whole thing to look contrived. But what could I do but plow ahead, nearly blubbering my response? "I—I have thought about that question many times … and … I've never said this in public, but … lately I have wondered…. Well, it's like this. For decades I haven't suffered. Not *really.* Yes, I'm a quadriplegic and that's hard, but it's mostly behind me. I'm used to it. I've almost forgotten what having hands that work feels like. But with this pain, it's—it's as though God is reintroducing me to suffering, like … I'm brand-new to it and have never experienced it before.

"Why? I don't know. Maybe—maybe He has allowed this so that what you've just heard—the last forty-five minutes—wouldn't come off as something trite, something rehearsed, or sound like a platitude. The Bible says, 'Not many of you should be teachers.' And perhaps this is why."

The classroom fell dead silent. Rising quietly from his perch on the front row, my wonderful Ken came up with a Kleenex—and I didn't even care that the students were watching me blow my runny nose. Anyway, I doubt that they minded.

You can't teach about suffering from a textbook. You can place yourself in front of a class, lecture, and even do a snappy PowerPoint, but how do you communicate truth so that words become a branding iron on a heart of soft wax? How else do you treat the subject of suffering? Sharing about suffering is like giving a blood transfusion … infusing powerful, life-transforming truths into the spiritual veins of another. And you can't do that with words only. Or, you shouldn't. How can you learn about suffering except by feeling the pain yourself? But mercifully, none of those sixty-five students had to break their necks that day or endure mind-bending pain. They just had to have faith that the tears were real … which proved that the Man of Sorrows really can redeem suffering.

For me and for them.

The Fight of My Life

So here I am gathering these thoughts and writing them down, working with an editor and starting a book when some would say that the timing is all wrong. "Wait awhile, Joni," they say. "Get some perspective. Conserve your energy. Concentrate on getting better."

Famous military leaders who write their memoirs are usually retired, but I'm still in the battle. Storied generals like Grant, Lee, Pershing, Eisenhower, Montgomery, and Churchill wrote after years of reflection. (I have a mental picture of a wicker rocking chair on an old-style front porch, with a light spring breeze carrying the scent of lilacs and teasing the corners of a writing tablet.) But I'm penning these words in the midst of hostilities, while the dust and smoke of war still drift over the battlefield.

In fact, I find myself in the fight of my life. I'm in the thick of it, as they say, and honestly have no idea how long this struggle will continue or how and when it will be resolved.

As I said, it's an unlikely time to write a book on healing.

To this very moment my great adversary is not the garden variety of aches and hurts associated with quadriplegia. No, this is something new and malevolent that has intruded into my life. It manifested first as a driving lance of pain in my neck. And just as I began to "reconcile myself" to that field of battle, a new, even fiercer attack broke out on a new front—my lower back. The persistent attacks of physical agony I have experienced over the last two years are beyond anything I could have imagined.

Words truly fail me.

After keeping me in the hospital for days and putting me through what seemed like every test known to man, doctors have at last discovered the culprit—or one of the culprits. It is a fracture in my sacrum—that large, triangular bone at the base of the spine. No wonder I've been in such a state! No wonder those fiery fingers radiate across my abdomen. The fact is, every moment I've been sitting up, I've actually been sitting on the injury itself.

Since remaining upright in my wheelchair for any length of time hasn't been possible, I've been working from a little bed in my office. Some days I do attempt to sit up for as long I am able, trying to complete as much work as I possibly can before pain drives me back to bed.

As you might imagine, it has complicated everything I do by a factor of ten. Here's one small example.

Not long ago I was sitting in my studio, attempting to record my *Joni and Friends* weekly radio program, an activity I have enjoyed for decades. On this occasion, however, I found myself with a very troubling choice: I could cinch my corset extra tight, enabling me to breathe properly in order to talk, but also greatly increasing my pain. Or, I could loosen the corset, lessening the pain, but making it a struggle to record. So I did both. It was read a page or two, stop, tighten the corset, then read again, then loosen it again. I got it done, but it all seemed so very slow and took so long.

The truth is, over this past year I've endured some of the most difficult days and weeks of my life—rivaling those early days in the Baltimore hospital after my injury.

An Honest Fear

Is my life beginning to unravel? Have I reached a limit in what I can endure? Have my friends and coworkers and—God forbid—my husband reached a limit in what *they* can endure for my sake? How much longer can I—can *they*—go on like this? These are the questions that plague me.

Finally, after all these years, I'm honestly beginning to wear people out. These are the people—around eight or so—who graciously offer to get me up in the morning—or in the case of Judy and my husband, Ken, help me through the night. It used to be that only my husband helped me turn in bed in the evening, and often, I didn't need his assistance through the night. He would put me up on my side, tuck my pillows, and then I'd comfortably sleep straight through until morning.

That doesn't work anymore.

Neither do muscle relaxers. Or Advil PM. Or even Vicodin. Or (and I'm sorry to say this) even stronger drugs than that.

I despise taking medication. Born of my mother and father's sturdy stock, I'm a little bit of German and a wee bit Scotch-Irish, with some Swedish thrown in for good measure. It's a solid constitution, my family line. For all my years (and I learned this from my parents), I took some pride in the fact that I could push through pain relying on only an aspirin or two. That's just the way I was made; that's the way I handled pain.

The medications don't work very long, anyway—and the side effects can sometimes be worse than the original affliction. It's a little like those

TV commercials that promise your skin will be silky smooth with this particular medicine—but take it only upon the risk of kidney disease, liver failure, dry mouth, nausea, and thoughts of suicide! Who wants nice skin after *that?!*

Seriously, nothing seems to work. Almost like clockwork, I wake up at 2 a.m. with searing pain in my lower back—particularly in the *quadratus lumborum* and the *iliopsoas.* (I know my muscle groups.) For the layman, it translates into the left lower back above my hip along with the left abdomen and inside of my thigh. It probably doesn't mean much to you, but those parts of my body—paralyzed as I am with no feeling in the rest of my limbs—in the wee small hours of the morning come alive with throbbing pain.

Sometimes I can get back to sleep. Most times I bite my lip until my whimpering can be heard by Ken who, unfortunately, now must sleep in a bedroom adjacent to the one we've shared for years. That's when he shuffles in, bleary-eyed and trying hard to not awaken himself too much so he can get back to sleep. Then on automatic pilot, he turns me. It used to be on my other side, but I can't tolerate that anymore. Now I go on my back for a couple hours. Then it's up again at 4 a.m., and hopefully that'll keep me until my girlfriends arrive at 7:30 a.m.

It never used to be this way. Honestly.

I never used to keep that kind of sleep schedule. I never used to whine. I never used to wake up wondering if I'd be able to get out of bed. Most of all, I never remember being this anxious or fearful. Some of it is understandable, but I suspect most of it is a side effect of the medications.

This is why I'm afraid I'm wearing out my friends. And my husband. Now when my girlfriends begin my exercise routine in the morning it involves at least an extra hour of stretching and pulling my muscles. "Oh, could you please pull on my back muscle? Like, angle your hand toward the headboard and … that's it…. Kind of rake-up my back with your fingers…. Gee, I can't quite feel that…. Can you dig in harder?"

They give me odd looks now. It used to be fun getting me up. We would sing. We would say to each other, "We get to go work for Jesus today!" But these days, we all just do the best we can.

But one thing *is* better.

We are all much more dependent on God for help.

And for sanity itself.

Because I have never been more aware that I am a target of the Devil and his hordes.

A Target

The adversary knows very well what my example of trust and confidence in God has meant to Christians throughout the years, from the time I published my first book, *Joni*, back in 1976 through the present. Has Satan read my books? I seriously doubt it—there's way too much Jesus in those pages for his liking. Nevertheless, he knows my love for the Savior and hates me for it.

My enemy has most probably assigned some captain in his lowerarchy of hell to harass me. My wicked adversary knows I have at least become accustomed to quadriplegia. He recognizes that total and permanent paralysis is no longer the struggle it used to be for me. He is aware that my profound disability has helped me develop the prized characteristic of needing God desperately when I wake up in the morning.

And quite frankly, he despises that.

He hates knowing that my trust in God resounds to the Father's glory. He detests thinking of my increased eternal capacity for worship and joy in heaven as a reward for my perseverance these forty-plus years in my wheelchair. He loathes the way my fellowship with Christ in His sufferings turns up the wattage on the Savior's glory. He considers it odious that I have yielded to the Hebrews 12–type discipline of the Lord in years past, and he sneers as he watches me "walk" deeper into that fellowship of suffering with Jesus.

It makes him sick.

Hence his full-on attack on my body, mind, and spirit, and on my friends who love me and help me. It's war—and like all war, it isn't pretty.

But there's something earthy about my response to God that further sickens Satan. I believe he views disabilities as his last great stronghold to defame the good character of God. Suffering is that last frontier he exploits to smear God's trustworthiness. The Devil relishes inciting people to complain, "How could a good God allow my child to be born with this horrible defect?" and asking, "How can I trust a God who would permit cancer to take my husband of only six months?" or wondering, "Why would I believe in a God who includes Alzheimer's and autism in His plans for people?"

My adversary knows that the Lord has used my personal testimony many times, in many ways, in many nations to push back dark thinking like that. He's certainly cognizant that the ministry of Joni and Friends has been used of God to promote His grace and goodness among the suffering in some of the darkest corners of our world. He knows I'm well aware that we wrestle not against the flesh and blood of disease and disability, but against powers and principalities that rub their hands in glee as they crush the hopes of disabled people, pushing them deeper into despair and discouragement (Eph. 6:12).

Little wonder I've got such a large target on my *quadratus lumborum.*

Battlefield Jesus

Does this chapter surprise you a little? Did you flip back and check the title page to see if you had the right author?

Do you find yourself objecting, perhaps, to the battlefield imagery I've employed to describe my life as is? Could it be you've never quite pictured your walk with Jesus in such terms?

Here at our ministry we refuse to present a picture of "gentle Jesus, meek and mild," a portrait that tugs at your sentiments or pulls at your heartstrings. That's because we deal with so many people who suffer, and when you're hurting hard, you're neither helped nor inspired by a syrupy picture of the Lord, like those sugary, sentimental images many of us grew up with. You know what I mean? Jesus with His hair parted down the middle, surrounded by cherubic children and bluebirds.

Come on. Admit it: When your heart is being wrung out like a sponge, when you feel like Morton's salt is being poured into your wounded soul, you don't want a thin, pale, emotional Jesus who relates only to lambs and birds and babies.

You want a warrior Jesus.

You want a battlefield Jesus. You want His rigorous and robust gospel to command your sensibilities to stand at attention.

To be honest, many of the sentimental hymns and gospel songs of our heritage don't do much to hone that image. One of the favorite words of hymn writers in days gone by was *sweet*. It's a term that doesn't have the edge on it that it once did. When you're in a dark place, when lions surround you, when you need strong help to rescue you from impossibility, you don't want "sweet." You don't want faded pastels and honeyed softness.

You want mighty. You want the strong arm and unshakable grip of God who will not let you go—no matter what.

For instance, I absolutely love that beautiful old hymn (a great favorite of my parents) "I Come to the Garden Alone." Remember the verse that says, "He speaks and the sound of His voice is so sweet, the birds hush their singing"? It's a nice sentiment, and I'm aware that a thought like that can provide comfort. But it's really just a reinforcement of a romanticized nineteenth-century image. We have gilded the real Jesus with so much "dew on the roses" that many people have lost touch with Him—or simply turned away.

Why do some people gravitate to a sentimental picture? Well, think about it: A sugar-coated Christ requires nothing from us—neither conviction nor commitment. Why? Because it's an image that lacks truth and power.

We have to try to change that picture.

And the only way to do it is to think about the resurrection.

Sure, romanticists try to color the resurrection with lilies and song-birds, but lay aside the emotions and think of the facts for a moment: A man, stone-cold dead—a cadaver of gray, cold flesh, really—rose up from His slab and walked out of His grave.

Friend, that's almost frightening. There's nothing sugar-coated about it. And the powerful thing is that it accurately describes what Jesus did. That reality has power; it's truth that grips you. Some people believe Jesus came to do sweet, pleasant things, like turning bad people into nice people. Not so. As someone once said, our Lord and Savior came to turn dead people into living ones—and there's nothing sentimental about that.

At different times in my life I've enjoyed the old pictures of Jesus cradling cute lambs or walking around with blow-dried hair, clad in a white robe looking like it just arrived from the dry cleaner. But these days, these warfare days, those old images just don't cut it for me. I need a battlefield Jesus at my side down here in the dangerous, often messy trenches of daily life. I need Jesus the rescuer, ready to wade through pain, death, and hell itself to find me, grasp my hand, and bring me safely through.

There will be a time very soon, I hope, when I will once again enjoy the casual stroll through the garden with Him, admiring the dew drops on the roses. But for right now, if I am to "endure hardship … like a good soldier" as 2 Timothy 2:3 mandates, I need a comrade in arms, a strong commander to take charge of my private war.

And that is exactly who He is, and what He has done.

Battle Zone

The book of James says: "Is any one of you sick? He should call the elders of the church to pray over him and anoint him with oil in the name of the Lord" (James 5:14).

Of course I had read that passage scores of times, and although I wasn't "sick," I wanted to do anything—everything I was supposed to do in this fierce battle—to obey Scripture. And so not long ago, after Sunday services on a bright sunny afternoon when I was still in bed in pain, Pastor Bob and our small group of elders entered my bedroom. They looked so large and out of place! Little did they know they had entered a war zone. (It happens every time you want to obey Scripture.)

As they opened their Bibles, I could feel dark spirits retreating—spirits of discouragement and doubt that had harassed and haunted me over the past few days. But with these Christian men—my husband, Ken, included—I felt safe for the first time. They read Scriptures, prayed, and then pulled out a small vial of oil.

When Pastor Bob approached the bed, I asked if he would give me a blessing at the close of his prayer for my healing—the sign of the cross on my forehead. Growing up as a Reformed Episcopalian, I knew this to be an outward physical symbol of, well … a seal, a kind of amen. *So be it. Let it be as the Lord wills.*

Bob prayed: "Lord God, You can, with a thought, simply take this pain of Joni's away, and so we pray that in the name of the Father, the Son, and the Holy Spirit that You would heal Joni of this long and tiring ailment." And at that he touched my forehead with oil and sealed his prayer.

That's right. It would only take a thought toward me, Lord. Just a thought from You.

The whole idea of the ease and simplicity with which God could touch me and release me from pain comforted me greatly. A fresh peace settled over the bedroom—a peace I had not sensed in days. Dark spirits of disappointment with God had vanished and my confidence in Him had been refreshed.

At that point Elder Dave kneeled by my bed and began singing a song that addressed one of the fears I had struggled with over the past day or so:

> *He who began a good work in you*
> *He who began a good work in you*

Will be faithful to complete it
He'll be faithful to complete it
He who started a work
Will be faithful to complete it in you[1]

I chimed in on harmony and we sang out the old Steve Green chorus for all it was worth.

Because who can live without purpose? Who can survive without a reason to live? If you are God's servant—and you are—you have been given a command. Many commands. And if He asks you to do something (and He has), you've just been given a reason for living every morning when you wake up. God who began a good work in me *will complete it!* Pastor Bob flipped his Bible open to Psalm 57:2–3 and read it as though it were a benediction: "I cry out to God Most High, to God, who fulfills [His purpose] for me. He sends from heaven and saves me, rebuking those who hotly pursue me."

I had been hotly pursued long enough by those dark spirits. And by the time my pastor and elders left, Ken and I were determined to look for God's redemption in my pain. For pain is a bruising of a blessing; but it *is* a blessing nevertheless. It's a strange, dark companion, but a companion—if only because it has passed through God's inspecting hand. It's an unwelcome guest, but still a guest. I know that it drives me to a nearer, more intimate place of fellowship with Jesus, and so I take pain as though I were taking the left hand of God. (Better the left hand than no hand at all.)

Perhaps the simple realization of something so redemptive is healing enough.

I don't know when this season of pain will be over. Maybe, in God's grace and wisdom, He'll say, "Enough!" and banish the pain within the hour. Or maybe He'll say, "Enough!" allowing me to step out of this long-disabled, deteriorating temporary housing into my "building from God, an eternal house in heaven, not built by human hands" (2 Cor. 5:1).

In the meantime, these afflictions of mine—*this very season of multi-plied pain*—is the background against which God has commanded me to show forth His praise. It's also that thing that I am to reckon as "good and acceptable and perfect," according to Romans 12. God bids me that I not only seek to accept it, but to *embrace* it, knowing full well that somewhere way down deep—in a secret place I have yet to see—lies my highest good.

Yes, I pray that my pain might be removed, that it might cease; but more so, I pray for the strength to bear it, the grace to benefit from it, and the devotion to offer it up to God as a sacrifice of praise. My strength in prayer these days is scant—I'll confess that. So for all the concentration I can muster in prayer, I must not dissipate it in seeking physical blessings only. Rather, I must spend a good portion of it seeking spiritual growth and praying for Christ's kingdom to go forth into this dark world. For such prayers are a way for me to know God and to know Him deeper, higher, richer, wider, and fuller—*much* fuller than if I comfortably cruised through life in my wheelchair.

To this point, as I pen this chapter, He has chosen not to heal me, but to hold me.

The more intense the pain, the closer His embrace.

That's one of the truths I'd like to speak to, God helping me, in the following pages.

Two

God and Healing: What's the Real Question?

There is a war going on. All talk of a Christian's
right to live luxuriously "as a child of the King"
in this atmosphere sounds hollow—especially
since the King himself is stripped for battle.
—John Piper

In the first and second decades of my paralysis, there were seasons during which my yearning for complete healing and a return to life-as-it-was gripped my heart. It's not that those desires have gone away in this, my fifth decade in a wheelchair; it has more to do with a change in my perspective.

In the first place, any concept of "normal" is now something so long ago and far away that it seems more like a distant dream. A pleasant dream, yes, but one that has gradually, gently faded through the years, like a well-loved snapshot in an old photo album. After forty-plus years of quadriplegia, it's hard to say what a normal life for me would be.

For another thing, as I have mentioned, I find myself in a whole new phase of the battle. It's not so much the wistful disappointments or occasional frustrations I'm dealing with now, it's the seemingly ceaseless attacks—wave after wave after wave of throbbing in my lower back and hip. Now when I think of "healing," it's more in the form of asking my Father for relief from the intensity of the suffering rather than the ability to pick a flower, ride a horse, or dance across a field of clover.

Relief from chronic pain—even though I remain paralyzed—would be blissfully, peacefully, joyously "normal" for me these days ... and all I could ask for. I don't remember where I saw the following Mary Jane Iron quote, but it comes pretty close to my take on "normal":

> Normal day, let me be aware of the treasure you are.... Let me not pass you by in quest of some rare and perfect tomorrow. One day I shall dig my nails into the earth, or bury my face in my pillow, or stretch myself taut, or raise my hands to the sky and want, more than all the world, your return.

That's my take on normal.

Come to think of it, I'm not even a "normal" quad. I have now exceeded the expected lifespan of a person with my level of injury and paralysis. The bare, unadorned fact is this: Many people in my condition simply don't live as long as I have lived. So my thoughts haven't been so much on picking up the old life on my feet I left behind in 1967, as much as stepping into the new life and body that await me.

Longings? Yes, my heart is as filled with longing as it was when I was in my twenties, yearning for the simple pleasures of a body that works the way it was intended. But now I am much closer to my new body of the Joni-that-will-be than I am to the healthy young woman's body of the Joni-that-was, injured in that diving accident.

Oh ... and what *will be* is far, far better than *what was*.

My desires have settled in on heaven and the immediate presence of my Lord Jesus. And why not? The Bible says I'm already a citizen of heaven; I don't need to update my passport or fill out any forms or change of address cards. The Bible says I'm already raised with Christ, seated with Him in heaven; I won't have to "find my place" when I get there because my place has already been reserved. It's "an inheritance that can never perish, spoil or fade—kept in heaven for [me]." Hooray for 1 Peter 1:4!

The Bible says that Jesus has, in His Father's house, prepared a room for me where I can see Him every day. I won't need MapQuest directions to find some lonely, heavenly mansion on a back street of some distant planet.

As with those men and women in the book of Hebrews who were trying to deal with persecution and the loss of so many precious earthly things, I am "longing for a better country—a heavenly one" (Heb. 11:16). And I have the firm assurance (you have no idea how firm, and how assuring) that God "has prepared a city for [me]."

What a city it will be! If you take the description of New Jerusalem in the book of Revelation quite literally rather than symbolically (I do, but suit yourself), it will be like a huge, radiant, translucent, impossibly beautiful cube floating over New Earth, measuring fifteen hundred miles in each direction and flashing like a great diamond in an ocean of light. And I can say with confidence that there won't be one wheelchair ramp or set of instructions in Braille or handicapped parking space in the whole city! In fact, if there's a fifteen-hundred-mile spiral staircase from the lowest level to the top, I'm going to run it every morning—before breakfast! (Can you even imagine? Around and around, never tiring, racing with the angels, bathed in colors beyond the spectrum, climbing from glory to glory!)

So when I think of physical healing for myself, it isn't in the same way I once considered it and longed for it.

Nevertheless, I've had to deal with those questions all of my life. We at Joni and Friends answer countless phone calls and letters and emails and spend many hours counseling with people for whom physical healing is very, very much something uppermost in their minds.

In the few pages of this brief chapter I'd like to land on what I consider to be the central question about miraculous healing. The way I see it, the question has never really been "*Can* God heal?"

Of course He can.

Everyone who believes in God will acknowledge that. This is the mighty One, the all-powerful Creator and sustainer of the universe, whose arm "is not too short to save, nor his ear too dull to hear" (Isa. 59:1). And our Lord Jesus, who solemnly pledged never to leave us or forsake us, didn't lose any of His love or compassion or healing power when He left earth to ascend to His Father. Yes, our great and magnificent God can heal anyone, anywhere, at any time, of any affliction.

Period.

End of sentence.

Nor is the question, "*Does* God heal today, in the twenty-first century?" Absolutely, He does. Every time you bounce back from the flu or heal from a surgery, that's God performing His Psalm 103:3 thing; no matter what kind of illness or disease we may rise above, it's *His* power that's accomplished it. Besides, how absurd it would be to say that He somehow went out of the miracle business after the last page of the book of Acts. Who can deny the reports of miraculous healing among God's children from every corner of the globe? What's more, who would *want* to? I have a God who certainly intervenes in all sorts of impossible situations in today's world, doing those things that only He can do to accomplish His purposes. There are far too many in our very midst who have experienced such miraculous healings for us to peremptorily write them off. Many such testimonies come from people who are mature in the faith and blessed with godly wisdom—and many are from the field of medicine itself.

No, miracles did not suddenly disappear after the apostolic age. However, we need to remember that miracles also were God's way of "authenticating" the true ministry of genuine apostles during the early days of the church. (There really were an awful lot of phony apostles running around back then!) The apostle Paul claimed that the church was able to know he was for real, and not phony, because of his lifestyle and "the things that mark an apostle—signs, wonders and miracles" (2 Cor. 12:12). So I have to bring a little balance to this point about miracles happening whole-scale nowadays. Wonders of healing were God's way of spotlighting those men that He raised up to begin and lead the church. And those men healed the sick big time!

The Real Question

But that was then. Nowadays, the *real* question, of course, is not whether God can heal or does heal; it is whether or not God *wills* to heal all those who truly come to Him in faith. In other words, is it always a given that He will say yes to our requests for healing? Is it a sure thing, a slam-dunk that miraculous healing is always His first and best option?

Some assert that very thing and insist that if you aren't experiencing this healing, it's only because you lack the necessary faith or perhaps have some hidden sin in your life. Others still insist that, no, miraculous healing belonged to another era, and we ought not to expect or even seek such divine intervention.

Let me state my answer to the question—the real question—in just twelve words. It's not a conclusion I have come to lightly; I have firmly arrived in this place after forty years of paralysis and decades of working with disabled and suffering people around this world.

Here is what I believe: *God reserves the right to heal or not ... as He sees fit.*

There are times when I feel almost sure I know what would be best in a given situation. *Lord, touch this woman's body and raise her up! Lord, heal this child! Lord, relieve this man's pain! Lord, reverse the effects of this terrible disease!*

But the fact is I only know so much, I only understand so much, I only see so much, and I only grasp so much of what I do see. With Paul, I sometimes have to cry out, "Oh, the depth of the riches of the wisdom and knowledge of God! How unsearchable his judgments, and his paths beyond tracing out!" (Rom. 11:33).

Not long ago, the words of this old hymn drifted into my mind:

> *I am not skilled to understand*
> *What God has willed, what God has planned;*
> *I only know at His right hand,*
> *Stands One who is my Savior!*[1]

Ah, there are many things that God has revealed—things I *do* know and understand. But there are many more things that He has not chosen to reveal yet and may not reveal this side of heaven. And one of those things is why He sometimes chooses to step in and supernaturally heal one person and not another.

But as you are no doubt aware, there are branches of Christendom in which individuals really do think they are "skilled to understand what God has willed, what God has planned" when it comes to sickness and disease. They will tell you that it's always God's will and desire to heal, and that if you're not experiencing that healing, then there's something wrong with *you* and with your faith.

I think back to a television interview I gave several years ago. It's not often that I feel uneasy in participating in a live, on-camera conversation. But this was one experience I will never forget.

I don't need to give the name of the popular Christian TV host, but suffice to say, our televised conversation didn't go very well. From the moment the floor director counted down the final seconds and the light on the camera clicked to bright red, I felt an unmistakable uneasiness. The questions were pointed and abrupt—occasionally rude.

As I look back, the whole scene seems surreal to me—and not like an interview at all. I felt more like a witness being cross-examined by a crafty lawyer. It was perfectly obvious what he *wanted* me to say. He was trying to get me to state that decades of quadriplegia were actually a result of my lack of faith. In other words, God had wanted to heal me all along, and I really could have been healed—if only I had "believed for it."

But I wasn't going to say any such thing. It wouldn't be true.

So I stood firm on Ephesians 1 and other Scriptures that confirm God works everything in accordance with His plan. And that plan often (actually, *most* often) allows for suffering or quadriplegia to continue for good and well-considered reasons that we often can't understand or discern this side of heaven.

The TV host didn't seem impressed with this line of reasoning. He had already made up his mind that he knew better, that it was always God's will to heal, and that the problem was all with me. So he listened woodenly as I spoke, mostly without comment, until the interview drew to a close. Then he turned to address the small studio audience and the camera, a window to who knows how many people watching their televisions at that moment.

He explained to his viewers that while it was obvious that Joni hadn't been healed of her infirmities, they, the viewers, *could* be. With confession of sin and enough faith to believe, they could experience what Joni had sadly not experienced. The people in the television audience who obeyed the correct formula could be—*should* be—healed.

Before I could jump in or speak a word in my own defense, the cameras turned to another segment on the studio stage. The red light on the camera blinked off. The interview was over.

I couldn't believe what had just happened to me! Had this Christian TV icon not read all the scriptural instances in which God specifically tells His followers—even followers with great faith—to *expect* hardship? Or how the sufferings of Christ are supposed to overflow into our lives? Had he never read in Acts 14 that we must go through many hardships to enter the kingdom of God? And that's just scratching the surface of this New Testament teaching!

The man may have had a huge ministry and millions of viewers, but he was *wrong*. God is God, and it is He and He alone who decides who will be healed and who will not. Yes, faith is vital to everything, and "without faith it is impossible to please Him." But faith's focus must always be Jesus Christ—and nobody draws close to Christ who doesn't first share in Christ's sufferings. Just stop a minute and consider these awesome words from the apostle Peter, who wrote, "To this you were called, because Christ suffered for you, leaving you an example, that you should follow in his steps" (1 Pet. 2:21). Christ and the manner in which He approached suffering is to be our focus, *especially* when the weight of our cross seems overwhelming. Man, it takes real faith to follow our suffering Savior's example!

Besides, at the end of the day, it's not a question of who has the most faith, but what God in His wisdom, love, and sovereignty chooses to do.

A Letter from Linda

Believe me, I know this is no mere academic discussion or idle talking point in some seminary cafeteria. Every day countless suffering, brokenhearted people spread their requests, hopes, and longings concerning these questions before the throne of heaven.

Here at Joni and Friends, as I mentioned, I receive so many letters from people who are struggling with blindness, encroaching disease, disability from injury, or maybe those with babies who have been born with a severe handicap. My heart aches with each such letter or email.

A woman named Linda recently wrote that she had taken her little boy with a brittle bone disease to a healing crusade. And even though she and her husband prayed, nothing happened at that crusade. It had been quite awhile, and their child was still struggling with this painful disability. In her letter to me, Linda confessed that the whole incident with the "healer" had nearly shipwrecked her faith.

As I have stated, at times of His choosing, God certainly does intervene and heal. But it's also true that even though multitudes of devoted, good-hearted Christians pray in great faith, many eyes will stay blind. Many babies will die at birth. Many cancers will not be eradicated until that once-and-forever healing of a new body and a new life in Christ's presence. And many paraplegics and quadriplegics like me will never regain the use of legs or arms or hands that don't work.

The Bible simply doesn't teach that God will always heal those who come to Him in faith. He sovereignly reserves the right to heal or not heal, as He sees fit. Even when Jesus walked the earth, only a small number of people—those who happened to be in His immediate vicinity—were healed. Yes, He fed four thousand people, and five thousand at another time. But many in Israel still went hungry. He drove out demons wherever He went, but many demons remained entrenched. He raised several people from the dead, but it was really only a few, and even those died later on.

In my conversation with Linda I encouraged her to look at the first chapter of Mark's gospel. After word spread throughout Capernaum about Jesus' healing Simon's mother-in-law, the whole town brought their sick and lame outside Simon's home. Long after sunset, Jesus was still preaching the gospel and backing up His words by healing people with diseases and illnesses. And then it says the next day, very early in the morning, those people returned, bringing still more friends and more relatives who needed healing.

Jesus, however, was nowhere around.

Simon and his companions went to look for Him, and when they found Him, probably somewhere on the hill above Capernaum, praying, they said to Him, "Jesus, everyone is looking for You." Translation: *"There are lots more people who need healing. In fact, there are some really heartbreaking situations. You've only scratched the surface!"*

Now you might imagine that Jesus, upon hearing this, would have jumped to His feet, gathered up His robe, and gone hurrying back down the hill to all those needy people who were waiting for Him—waiting in faith! But not so. If you read Mark 1:38, you can almost picture His rising slowly to His feet, dusting off His robe, and then replying after a moment's thought: "Let's go somewhere else—to the nearby villages—so I can preach the gospel there, because that's why I have come."

As time has gone by since her disappointment at the healing crusade, Linda has begun to see that God is a lot higher, a lot bigger, and a lot more holy and sovereign than she ever realized. She's learning that her God is in control—not only for the good of a little boy who still has brittle bone disease, but for her good as well.

Will she give up, then? Will she stop praying for her boy's healing? Of course not. The gospel of Luke reminds us to pray always and not give up.[2] Jesus Himself urges us to keep on asking, keep on seeking, and keep on knocking. God, in His grace and compassion, could yet choose to heal the boy. *But it will be in His time, and in accordance with His mighty purposes.* And for Linda, though her heart aches, that's good enough.

In an insightful little volume penned over eighty years ago (I'll reference this more completely in the next chapter), a missionary named Henry Frost wrote about several of his friends who had prayed for healing but were content to leave the results in the hands of God. In fact, some of these were healed while others weren't. Did these suffering people all pray in assurance? Yes, Frost noted, but it wasn't so much an assurance that their specific prayer would be answered. *It was rather an assurance of the power, love, and wisdom of God.*

He wrote: "The general attitude of those who prayed, and hence, of those who exercised faith, was this: They believed that God could heal; that He would heal if it was for His glory and for the good of the person who was sick; and finally, that He could be trusted implicitly to do what was right and best."

Frost went on to add: "Those who prayed left the issue of their prayers with the heavenly Father in child-like confidence, repeating the prayer for healing until His will was known, and accepting the answer when it came, whatever it was, with submissive and trustful praise."[3]

God's Desires and My Desires

Some time ago at a Joni and Friends event, I met a man in a wheelchair named Lloyd. He had been in a car accident seven years previous and, as a result, was left a paraplegic—with no use of his legs. As the evening unfolded, I could tell by the expression on Lloyd's face that something was deeply moving him. Just seeing and interacting with other people more disabled than he seemed to be helping his heart.

When the event was over, I grabbed the chance to speak with him. "Well," he told me, "I've been to three healing crusades and ... *this* is much more meaningful. I need to get involved in more stuff like this."

Lloyd and I had a chance to talk about what happens at healing crusades. I shared that at one time, years ago, I too had been desperate to get healed. My sister Jay and I heard that Kathryn Kuhlman, a famous faith healer, was coming to the Washington, D.C., Hilton ballroom. Stories had reached us about cancer-ridden people who'd been cured in Philadelphia, Pennsylvania, at one of her crusades. I wondered if I should go to the healing service in Washington, D.C.

One morning, when Jay was putting my legs through my range-of-motion exercises, Ernest Angley came on television. He was an odd sort of man who wore a bad toupee and ill-fitting suits, and Jay and I enjoyed his antics. My sister and I stopped and watched as people dropped their crutches or got up out of their wheelchairs, many raising their hands and declaring they were free from pain.

"Do you think God could heal you?" Jay asked, staring at the screen.

"Maybe it *is* time," I replied. And so, wondering if this might be an answer to the prayers of many, we found our way to the Washington Hilton and the packed healing service in the big ballroom.

I remember the night so well. Miss Kuhlman breezed onto the stage under the spotlight in her white gown, and my heart raced as I prayed, *Lord, the Bible says You heal all our diseases. I'm ready for You to get me out of this wheelchair. Please, would You?* But the spotlight always seems to be directed toward some other part of the ballroom where apparent healings were happening. Never did they aim the light at the wheelchair section where all the "hard cases" were: quadriplegics like me, stroke survivors, children with muscular dystrophy, and men and women sitting stiff and rigid from multiple sclerosis.

God answered. And again, His answer was no.

After the crusade I was number fifteen in a line of thirty wheelchair users waiting to exit at the stadium elevator, all of us trying to make a fast escape ahead of the people on crutches. I remember glancing around at all the disappointed and quietly confused people and thinking, *Something's wrong with this picture. Is this the only way to deal with suffering? Trying desperately to remove it? Get rid of it? Heal it?*

Lloyd asked me, "How did you resolve that, Joni?"

I took a deep breath and sat silent for a moment.

"Lloyd," I said slowly. "I did resolve it. I resolved the issue with one simple Bible verse. Psalm 37:4: 'Delight yourself also in the Lord, and He shall give you the desires of your heart.'"[4]

Lloyd shot me a quick look. I knew what he was thinking. It would seem like *that* kind of verse would be a guarantee of healing!

"I can read your thoughts, Lloyd," I said with a smile, "but let me explain."

And so, for the remaining time we talked, I reflected on how after that Katherine Kuhlman crusade, I had embarked on a quest to delight myself in the Lord. "I started reading the Bible more and praying and asking God to reveal Himself," I told him. "I asked Him to show me His heart, give me His passion for the lost, keep me from temptation, and help me be a better witness.

"In the process of my pursuit, I just ate God up. I made it my goal to simply delight myself in *Him*. And not with the purpose of holding back on a couple of desires I'd hoped He would quickly fulfill once I delighted myself in Him. No, I didn't center on what God could do for me. Not how He could please me, but how I could please Him. I kept putting my wants and wishes in check and, instead, made certain my goal was simply to enjoy the Lord being … the Lord! And you'll never guess what happened!"

Lloyd shook his head and didn't try to guess.

"God gave me the desires of my heart!" I said.

Lloyd looked at my wheelchair, then back at my face. He was listening very intently.

"It's true," I said. "He really did. The thing was, because I had delighted myself in God, He miraculously replaced my little private lists of wants and wishes with a list of His own. *His desires became mine.* And what are His desires? That the gospel go forth, that the kingdom be advanced, that the earth be reclaimed as rightfully His, that the lost get saved, that His glories be made known.

"That's when it hit me, Lloyd. My wheelchair was the key to seeing all this happen—especially since God's power always shows up best in weakness. So here I sit … glad that I have not been healed on the outside, but glad that I have been healed on the inside. Healed from my own self-centered wants and wishes."

It was then Lloyd's turn to take a deep breath, be quiet for a moment, look at his own wheelchair, and then … smile.

How Does He Care for Us?

Every now and then, as I mentioned in my introduction, I still meet people who want to pray for my physical healing.

As I've said, I never turn someone down who wants to intercede for me. But recently, when a woman named Karen asked if she could pray for me, I first asked her to pray specifically about things in my life that truly needed healing—such as my tendencies toward selfishness, my lazy attitude about important spiritual disciplines, and things like that.

I could tell that wasn't what Karen had in mind. She wanted to see me get up and *walk*. Right then. After we had prayed, she continued to press her point about God's care and compassion for "people like you, in your wheelchairs."

She pointed to 1 Peter chapter 5, where God tells us to cast all our anxiety on Him, because He cares for us.

"Joni," she said, "God doesn't want to hurt you. He wants to help you. That's in His nature. He'd go to any lengths to release you from severe pain and a difficult disability."

When Karen shared that with me, the first thing that came to mind was the way God cared for Timothy in the Bible. The text says that this young man had to deal with frequent illness, and there is no record that he found healing. Instead, the apostle advised him to use a little medicinal wine to settle his stomach.[5] God also cared for James, but James was run through with Herod's sword because of his testimony.[6] God cared for John, but allowed him to be exiled and left isolated on a lonely island.[7] He cared for Stephen, from the first stones that struck the young man's earnest, unmarred face to the last one that sent him out of his broken body.[8] He cared for Paul's companion Trophimus, whom the apostle had to leave behind sick in Ephesus—though he was desperately needed for ministry.[9]

While I'm not saying God enjoys watching us struggle, His Word clearly indicates He allows wounds to prick and pierce us. But that doesn't mean He has stopped caring. God expresses His care in different ways. As many have said so eloquently, sometimes He delivers us *from* the storm, and at other times He delivers us *through* the storm.

And even if the storm happens to take our earthly life, He delivers us safely into the best and most joyous place we could ever wish for in our most agonizingly beautiful dreams. Just look at what happened to Paul near the end of his life. While sitting in a dank prison, he writes confidently to his friend Timothy (in the last letter he would ever write), "The Lord will rescue me from every evil attack and will bring me safely to his heavenly kingdom" (2 Tim. 4:18). A short time later, a Roman soldier lifted his sword and, with a swift stroke, killed the old apostle. That was one evil attack from which God obviously *did not* rescue Paul. Instead, that Roman's sword became the blessed key which opened the latch on the pearly gates to welcome Paul into heaven! Just another example that healing and escape from suffering isn't always God's priority for us.

On other occasions when Paul sat in a prison cell, he no doubt cast all his anxiety on God and had confidence that God cared about his situation. In fact, the Lord Himself appeared to Paul and said, "Take courage! As you have testified about me in Jerusalem, so you must also testify in Rome."[10]

The Lord came to Paul. Spoke to Paul. Encouraged Paul. Isn't that proof that He cared? And yet after that encouraging visit by the Lord Himself, Paul remained in custody at least *two more years*. Did God stop caring for Paul during those twenty-four long months in confinement? Of course not. And God proves it by giving Paul the kind of peace that allowed him to write from his prison cell, "I have learned the secret of being content in any and every situation."[11]

Could God have caused Paul's chains to drop off and open the prison doors to allow him walk free? Who could doubt it? He did it for Paul and Silas in Philippi—with a great earthquake! He did it (twice) for the apostle Peter. *But was it any less of a miracle to meet with Paul in that dungeon and give Him a supernatural contentment in that place? Was that a somehow lesser thing?*

You may not be in prison (although you might), but you may be lying in a hospital bed, or a bed at home, struggling for weeks with being sick. Or you may still be laid up from your knee surgery or hip surgery. You might be struggling in your marriage with unhealthy and unhappy circumstances that have gone on for years.

Well, today grab hold of the truth of 1 Peter 5, and cast all your anxieties on the Lord. He may not miraculously touch your knee or hip, throw open the doors of the prison, instantly erase your migraine, raise you up tonight from your sick bed, lift you out of your wheelchair, or immediately change your spouse's heart. But He *will* give you contentment, deep and profound, in any and every situation.

Someone might ask, "Have you always had such contentment, Joni?" And I would have to answer no. I well remember the first Christmas I got out of the hospital, my first visit home since the accident. Depressed and frightened, I remember going to church with my family on Christmas Eve. One particular carol stands out in my mind. I remember singing, with tears falling from my eyes:

> *Hail the heav'n-born Prince of Peace!*
> *Hail the Son of Righteousness!*
> *Light and life to all He brings,*
> *risen with healing in His wings.*

When we got to that third verse of "Hark, the Herald Angels Sing," I thought, *I'm sure this Christmas season I'll get up out of my wheelchair—risen with healing in His wings!*

Little did I know (and I don't know if I would have understood even if you had explained it to me) that in due time, God would heal me—but on a level I would have never dreamed. Just two years later, on another Christmas, I found the very peace and contentment that had eluded me. I also found joy, simply because I had embraced His will for my life.

And what is His will?

That you and I be in the best position, the best place, the timeliest circumstance in which God can be glorified the most.

For me, that place just happens to be a wheelchair.

That happens to be my place of healing.

Don't Miss the Miracles All Around You

Many Christians don't see God in their trials. If no dramatic miracles seem to be happening—if the floods aren't receding or the cancer isn't in remission—they think God must not be at work. That's because they think of miracles as the sort Hollywood's special-effects wizards manufactured in the movie *The Ten Commandments.* "Those ten plagues on Egypt ... now that was God up to something!"

Well, yes. Thunder and hail, rivers of blood, armies of locusts, and frogs in Pharaoh's bed (to Yul Brynner's great discomfort) made for a great film back in the fifties. Ah, but if we could only watch the real movie of how God runs the world from behind the scenes!

Oh, the infinite complexity of it all! Talk about God doing miracles! Just think of the miraculous way He wrenches good out of evil, like blood from a turnip—the way God operates behind the scenes, always exploiting Satan's worst escapades. And think of the miraculous, divine balancing act of weather systems that assure the arrival of summer. Think of the way God even infiltrated grace and salvation behind the barbwire of Soviet death camps. And look at the miraculous way God rallies the exact number of white blood cells, calling each one into action to defeat your illness.

I tell you, if we could only watch the way God works behind the scenes, we would have a greatly expanded view of the miraculous. The superbly conceived, delicately balanced, invisible workings of our great God—this is the real drama.

Meanwhile, He just wants us to trust Him.

As Jesus told skeptical Thomas in John 20:29 right after the resurrection: "Because you have seen me, you have believed; blessed are those who have not seen and yet have believed."

So why do we still doubt? We know God is always shifting and pulling and pushing and making things happen behind the scenes. Why do we agonize? Why can't we trust Him? Why can't we rest in His "good, acceptable, and perfect will" for our lives? Each of us must experience a thousand miracles in our lives every day! Maybe it's because in our heads, we can't find mental wrapping paper wide enough to neatly package such truths. It takes faith to realize that our almighty God *is* moving miraculously in our lives every day.

Friend, our inability to comprehend something doesn't make it untrue or any less miraculous. Count His miracles today. Count the many narrow misses. Count the smiles and words of encouragement and expressions of gratitude sent your way today. Count the safety and well-being of your children and grandchildren. Count the miracle of being able to worship God freely in a country like this. Count the miracles of grace, of which 1 Peter 1:12 tells us that "even angels long to look into these things." And thank Him. Honestly, it'll be healing to your bones.

In John 14:12 Jesus said, "Anyone who has faith in me will do what I have been doing. He will do even greater things than these, because I am going to the Father."

I've found that an interesting thing takes place when you "fix your faith on Jesus." You begin praying and asking for the sorts of things that *He* wants accomplished rather than zeroing in exclusively on your own private prayer list. You pray for the success of the gospel, even for mountains to be moved that His word might go forth. You pray for despair and discouragement to be alleviated in ten thousand obscure places around the world. You pray for souls to be settled and for God's people to experience peace that is profound. You pray for lives to have intensity and depth; you pray for joy and peace in the church without a lot of parade and noise.

Those are among the greater miracles in which I move every day, and I would not trade them for the lesser miracle of being healed from quadriplegia.

Henry Frost concurred with this point of view. In his study of people in his own sphere who had prayed for healing but not received it, he noted that "special spiritual blessings were given to the persons who were permitted to be sick, and that most of the persons, if not all of them, were finally constrained to testify that they believed that the sickness had proved to be even better than health could have been."[12]

The veteran missionary and friend of Hudson Taylor added this notation:

> If I may be permitted to refer to my own experience in this connection, I would witness to the fact that the deepest, the most precious, and the most abiding spiritual lessons which God has been pleased to teach me were learned in consequence of enduring my various experiences of sickness. This last is particularly true in respect to the prayer-life, the praise-life, the life of dependence upon God, and the life which chooses to live not for the seen, but for the unseen, not for the temporal, but for the eternal....
>
> I feel it would have been nothing short of a calamity to have missed the physical suffering through which I have passed....
>
> I am positive that I have sometimes met with God's refusal to heal when I have been most in fellowship with Him.[13]

And so it has been in my life.

A no answer has purged sin from my life, strengthened my commitment to Him, forced me to depend on grace, bound me with other believers, produced discernment, fostered sensitivity, disciplined my mind, taught me to spend my time wisely … and widened my world beyond what I would have ever dreamed had I never had that accident in 1967.

My affliction has stretched my hope, made me know Christ better, helped me long for truth, led me to repentance of sin, goaded me to give thanks in times of sorrow, increased my faith, and strengthened my character. Being in this wheelchair has meant knowing *Him* better, feeling His pleasure every day.

If that doesn't qualify as a miracle in your book, then—may I say it in all kindness?—I prefer my book to yours.

THREE

HEALER ... AND LORD

Christ did die to destroy sickness, and He
will yet do it. But He does not say that
He will, in a perfect sense, do it now.
—Henry Frost

There are times when I have watched a healing service on TV as I'm being exercised, dressed, and lifted into my wheelchair.

It's a little bit of a surreal experience.

There I am, lying in bed, disabled and unable to care for myself, listening to the fiery message and watching people hobble on stage with crutches ... and then walk off without them.

"Jesus doesn't want you sick and disabled," the speaker will often thunder. "He wants to do for *you* what He's done for those you've seen today. You, too, can experience His healing power. Rest your faith on His promises!"

As I watch, I often think about other sick and disabled people all over the country who are viewing the same broadcast. What are they thinking? Are they asking themselves the same questions I asked years ago? Questions like, "Does God still heal people miraculously today? If so, does He want to heal all or just some? And what am I to think if my prayers for healing go unanswered, unlike the prayers of those I see on TV?"

As I mentioned in the previous chapter, one of the milestones for me in answering questions like that was running across a book by a man named Henry Frost, a Canadian missionary statesman of an earlier generation. His book *Miraculous Healing* was first published in 1931. A contemporary of the great missionary pioneer Hudson Taylor, Frost served as the first home director of the China Inland Mission (now Overseas Missionary Fellowship) for North America.

Miraculous Healing isn't a new book by any means. Nor does it read like this morning's newspaper. In fact, the language sounds rather stilted and out of date to our modern ears. But I doubt whether you'll ever find a more sensible and balanced treatment on the subject of divine healing. What first drew me to the book was the obvious fact that Henry Frost didn't seem to have any theological ax to grind. Rather than approaching the subject as a combatant for any particular point of view and armed with well-selected prooftexts, Frost maintained a gentle spirit and an open, inquiring heart.

Writing as an eyewitness, he examined situations where God does heal and then asked, "Now, what did all these people have, or do, in common? What keys can we find if we wish to be healed as well?" His conclusions aren't only helpful and interesting, but are firmly rooted in the pages of the Bible. This double-edged sword of Scripture and personal experience cuts through thickets of error and misconceptions to present one of the clearest discussions about miraculous healing I've ever heard.

You may have the opportunity to read the whole book for yourself—and I hope you do. But for those who might have difficulty with the outdated and sometimes technical language, allow me to give you some of its flavor in the next few pages—along with my own thoughts and experiences on several of his key points.[1]

1. **Jesus is just as concerned about our health and healing today as He was when He walked this earth.**

When it comes to seeking the Lord for physical healing—or endurance to bear up under suffering He has permitted to enter our lives—I can't help but think about the words Peter addressed to Jesus at a crucial point in our Lord's ministry. "Lord, to whom would we go? You have the words that give eternal life. We believe them, and we know you are the Holy One of God."[2]

We come to Jesus in our times of stress and heartache and pain and bewilderment. Where else would we turn? Where else could we go? If we belong to the Son of God, then our lives are all about Jesus. Yes, we look for help from earthly physicians, hospitals, medicines, physical therapists, and counselors. That's a given. But we ultimately look to Jesus. He is our Great Physician and *the source of all healing and help.*

If not Him, who else?

One translation of Hebrews 4:16 says, "So let us come boldly to the very throne of God and stay there to receive his mercy and to find grace to help us in our times of need."[3]

I like that phrasing, that we would go to the throne of God and *stay there* to receive the mercy and grace we seek. There is no better place to be in the entire universe.

Henry Frost writes:

> Christ in heaven has all power upon earth, and
> His present interest in the members of His body
> is as close and compassionate as it was when He
> was on earth amongst men.... If Jesus were on
> earth and I needed Him for healing, I should go
> to Him for this even as others went to Him; as

He is not on earth, I cannot go to Him in person;
nevertheless, I may reach Him by faith where
He is in heaven, and since He is not changed in
character, I may expect Him to heal where there
is need, even as He used to heal.[4]

"… It is my present, deep conviction that Christ does strengthen and heal, and that He is more often ready to do the one and the other for those who put their trust in Him than most Christians realize."[5]

Looking back on Jesus' earthly ministry, what do you think was on the Lord's heart when He healed those who were paralyzed? When He opened the eyes of the blind? What was the Lord feeling when He counseled the father of the little boy who was gripped by seizures?

There are those who point to such miracles as signs of Christ's lordship saying, "Jesus healed those people as evidence of His authority as the Son of God. By such power, He was proving He was Messiah."

They are right. But it's not as though Jesus only approached blind people and healed them to prove a point about Himself. No, God did not use helpless people to advance His own agenda. He did not enlist hurting men and women as "props" or audiovisual aids to teach an important lesson about Himself. Neither did He approach blind, deaf, or paralyzed people in an emotional vacuum.

How do I know? Scripture tells us. He was moved with compassion when He saw the hurting masses. Oh, I'm so glad for that! I could never imagine Jesus healing someone as if He were a mystic guru who stood there aloof and unemotional, "in touch with the universe," above and beyond humans. No, no. I can't imagine Him acting untouchable, saying, "Yes, I can heal you. Here, beg at My feet and let Me show you what it means to be the Messiah."

I've never pictured Jesus that way. When I read the many accounts of the Lord healing the sick and opening the eyes of the blind, He is pictured as being filled with compassion. That's why I'm convinced He didn't heal people only to prove a point about His being Messiah; He didn't look at men and women as guinea pigs for testing truth. He cared for them as His own. He considered them dear to His heart. He desired to work His will in their lives, not just for His benefit and others, but for the person He was healing. When He touched them with His love, He really meant it.

How much so? Early on in the book of Revelation, the Lord says, "I know your affliction." Elsewhere He says, "I have seen your affliction." And not just seeing or knowing; He is moved by your tears. Remember, He places your tears in His bottle (Ps. 56:8 KJV). Now there's a reason God's Word describes it that way—because in a bottle, our tears won't evaporate. They won't disappear. God's compassion is so great that He remembers your afflictions for all time.

What's more, in a bottle He can *weigh* your tears. Those tears represent how *long* you've suffered. Think of those times when the heartache seems to just go on forever. You wonder when it will ever end. When will you get relief? When Job first experienced loss in his life, he said, "The Lord gives and the Lord takes away; blessed be the name of the Lord." But then much later when the suffering hadn't let up but only got worse, Job said, "As surely as God lives, who has denied me justice, the Almighty, who has made me taste bitterness of soul" (Job 27:2). Right there shows you what chronic pain and heartache can do to you! But God understands that. And He doesn't just know about it, He cares. He's compassionate!

Thoughts like these help and comfort me when I need the healing touch of Jesus, when I need to feel His compassion and His heart. Lamentations 3:32–33 reveals the heart intent of Jesus. It says there, "Though he brings grief, he will show compassion, so great is his unfailing love. For he does not willingly bring affliction or grief to the children of men."

He does not *willingly*—that is, He doesn't from the heart—bring affliction or grief. Suffering may be a part of God's larger and most mysterious plan, but God's intention is always to demonstrate compassion and unfailing love that touches people at their deepest point of need.

This is the heart of the Healer. Praise His name!

Henry Frost wrote:

> Christ is the eternal Son of God, and He is in His divine attributes 'the same yesterday and today and forever' (Hebrews 13:8). If therefore He loved in the days of His flesh, He loves now; if He cared then, He cares now; if He healed then, He heals now. It does not necessarily follow that He will do now all that He did then, or that He will do what He does now in the same way as He did then, for His purposes in some things are different at present from what they were in the past. Nevertheless, *Christ is changeless in character,* and we may be sure that He is infinitely interested in us and concerned about us.[6]

Isn't that great to know during times when dark circumstances crowd in on us and we feel afraid?

My friend Stephanie is the mother of a disabled child and heads up a special-needs outreach within our denomination. Stephanie has known about my challenges with pain for some time now. And not long ago she thought of me when she was reading about Gideon in the book of Judges.

Stephanie wrote to tell me how she was particularly struck by this portion of the story that says:

> Now the camp of Midian lay below him in the valley. During the night the LORD said to Gideon, "Get up, go down against the camp, because I am going to give it into your hands. If you are afraid to attack, go down to the camp with your servant Purah and listen to what they are saying. Afterward, you will be encouraged to attack the camp."(Judg. 7:8–11)

Then she wrote me this most amazing insight. It was short and sweet, but very powerful (at least for me). Stephanie told me, "Joni, I guess what caught my attention was the phrase, *'If* you are afraid.'" God didn't chide Gideon for his fears; God didn't scold him. Instead, He anticipated those fears. And the Lord seemed to acknowledge that—in Gideon's fallen human frailty—he was going to be afraid. But instead of dismissing Gideon's fear, God provides a way out. A way of encouragement for him.

Oh, that spoke to me! I am so grateful that with this disability of mine, God knows my frame; He remembers that I am made out of dust.[7] He knows, He anticipates the fact that I'm going to be afraid. He understands there are times when I dread the fact that my pain medication is wearing off, that I can't do anything about it for another five or six hours.

I told Stephanie that and she replied with a fun little story. She said, "I used to work at the Helping Up Mission in Baltimore, Maryland, when I was a teenager, and I taught the preschool class. Each day they had to memorize a little Bible verse and received a ticket they could use at the mission store. One day the verse was,

'He cares for you,' from 1 Peter 5. One little girl, whose family situation was pretty rough, came up to me and proudly recited, 'He's *scared* for you.'

"To me, that sounded like an accurate translation, given her circumstances. Jesus took on her fear, so she didn't need to. So I didn't hesitate to give her the ticket for memorizing the verse."

Back in the Christmas season, we celebrated the glorious gift of God with us. Immanuel … God is *with* us. And He is our Wonderful Counselor who understands our circumstances—and us—so very deeply. Anticipating our fear, He provides a way out by inviting us to cast it all on Jesus, because no one cares about our fears like Him.

Friend, at times I live in dread of the pain that looms on the horizon. And maybe you struggle with that too. Well, "if you are afraid," be encouraged. In God's grace He foresees your fear and will always provide a way out of the fear. And I have Stephanie, the account of Gideon, and a little girl from the slums of Baltimore to thank for that reminder.

2. Yes, we are healed by His wounds—but not necessarily immediately.

All life, all healing, and all atonement flow from that fountain who is our Lord Jesus Christ. Where else would it come from?

In Isaiah 53:5, we read these words: "But he was pierced for our transgressions, he was crushed for our iniquities; the punishment that brought us peace was upon him, and by his wounds we are healed."

Yes, we can certainly see that our Lord's suffering and death has saved us from our sins and brought us peace with God. But did it also secure for us an unconditional, no-strings-attached guarantee for instantaneous physical healing?

It's true that disease flows from the curse God pronounced on us after Adam's rebellion. It is also true that Jesus came to reverse this curse. Does it follow, then, that Christians shouldn't have to put up with cancer, Down syndrome, Lyme disease, or Alzheimer's? We'd like to think that since Jesus came to take up our diseases, there should be healing for everything from migraines to menopausal sweats. But that's akin to saying, "There's an oak in every acorn—so take this acorn and start sawing planks for picnic tables." Or saying, "Congress just passed the Clean Water Act, so tomorrow morning Manhattan residents can start drinking from the East River." A century may pass before that oak is ready for lumbering—and purging industrial ooze out of a river will take decades.

So it is with Jesus' reversal of sin's curse (and the suffering that goes with it). What Jesus began doing to sin and its results won't be complete until the second coming. The purchase of salvation was complete and the outcome was settled with certainty (and note that the context of Isaiah 53:5 and 1 Peter 2:24 refers to deliverance from sin, not disease). But the *application* of salvation to God's people was anything but finished.

God "*has* saved" us, yet we are still "being saved" (1 Cor. 1:18). We are still on earth. This means we're still going to feel the influence of that old curse. At least until heaven where—what do you know—"we *will* be saved" (Matt. 24:13)!

First Corinthians 15:45 calls Jesus "the last Adam" who came to undo the curse triggered in the garden of Eden. But this summer you'll still be wrestling with weeds in your backyard, as well as a backache from all that hoeing. Only in paradise will it be said, "No longer will there be any curse" (Rev. 22:3). [8]

Theologian Richard Mayhue wrote: "Isaiah 53 primarily deals with the spiritual being of man. Its major emphasis is on sin, not sickness. It focuses on the moral cause of sickness, which is sin, and not on the immediate removal of one of sin's results—sickness."[9]

I have truly been healed by His wounds. He may yet choose to give me temporary deliverance and relief from my chronic pain, for which I would be most grateful. But whether He grants that or not, I know that complete healing is "just around the corner," in my Father's house. And how could I have ever had hope of even entering my Father's house apart from the blood of Jesus, shed on the cross for my eternal salvation?

3. Our Lord Jesus has varied purposes for His own.

Without a doubt, this to me is the strongest argument for trusting Jesus with our suffering.

Some of us will live long lives, mostly hale and hearty through all our years. Others of us will die relatively young, before we've lived out the expected span of years, or have to endure disabilities, frequent illness, physical weakness, or (in my present case) chronic pain. David had it right when he wrote: "But I trust in you, O LORD; I say, 'You are my God.' My times are in your hands" (Ps. 31:14–15).

My times … in His hand. That's just where I want my times to be. I can't imagine them anywhere else!

God has a purpose for my life, an intention He had in mind before the beginning of time—and certainly before I was ever that proverbial gleam in my daddy's eye.

Romans 8:29 says that "those God foreknew he also predestined to be conformed to the likeness of his Son, that he might be the firstborn among many brothers." Besides all the other reasons for my life, His highest purpose is that I might become gradually conformed to the image of His Son, who lives within me. And day by day He works in me and through me; I am His workmanship, as Ephesians 2:10 says, "created in Christ Jesus to do good works, which God prepared in advance for [me] to do."

As you may know from your own Bible study, that word "work-manship" in the original language, Greek, is *poiema*, from which we get our English word "poem."

He has a plan and purpose for my time on earth. He is the master artist or sculptor, and He is the one who chooses the tools He will use to perfect His workmanship. What of suffering, then? What of illness? What of disability? Am I to tell Him which tools He can use and which tools He can't use in the lifelong task of perfecting me and molding me into the beautiful image of Jesus? Do I really know better than Him, so that I can state without equivocation that it's always His will to heal me of every physical affliction? If I am His poem, do I have the right to say, "No, Lord. You need to trim line number two and brighten up lines three and five. They're just a little bit dark." Do I, the poem, the thing being written, know more than the poet?

If you want to see that point of view in spades, all you have to do is Google, "God wants you healed." In two clicks you'll see all the ministries and Web sites proclaiming God's blanket desire that everyone who calls on Him in faith will be made well and whole, free of injury and disease.

Here are some statements from just one such site—the first one I happened to open:

> So why aren't we seeing greater manifestations of His healing? Aren't people still suffering from sickness? Doesn't Jesus love people today just as much as He did when He walked the earth? Don't believers still need to see demonstrations of His power?

> YES! Not only do we need the healing power of God today, but God wants to release that power. Hallelujah! However, healing isn't up to God

alone. It isn't God who decides who gets healed
and who doesn't. That's a radical statement, but
it's true. And herein lies some of the greatest
obstacles to receiving God's healing power.[10]

So, "it isn't God who decides who gets healed and who doesn't"?
I'm sure that would be news to Him.

In other words, according to this author, God isn't the one who is
shaping me and forming me and conforming me? He isn't the one who
is using all the tools in His toolbox to make me most like Jesus and so
that I can bring Him maximum glory? I have to do that on my own?
It's up to me?

Horrible thought! How I would hate to bear that responsibility on
my own shoulders. I wouldn't last at that job for two minutes!

Really this is just the same old inexpressibly weary harangue I've
heard for decade upon decade. (I used to have more patience with it
than I feel these days.) I'm sure you've heard it too—and I've already
mentioned it earlier in the book: If you aren't well, if you are suffering
in any way, *you* are the one who is blocking that flow of healing power
because of *your* hidden sin or *your* lack of faith. Because God obviously
wants everyone well.

Believe me, I have seen the wreckage, heartbreak, confusion, guilt,
despair, and faith-destroying corrosive power of these hateful argu-
ments for more years and in more lives than I care to count.

Yes, Jesus is and always will be the fountainhead, source, and limit-
less artesian well of healing, forgiveness, redemption, and life.

Henry Frost, writing eighty-plus years ago, even suggested that as
the world's cultures move further and further from the foundations
of God's Word and apostasy increases (a picture of our world today?),
Christ may manifest Himself with even more miraculous signs and
healings.

It is therefore true that there are large parts of the
world where healing miracles, in proof of a living and all powerful Christ, may well be looked
for; and it may confidently be anticipated, as the
present apostasy increases, that Christ will manifest His deity and lordship in increasing measure
through miracle-signs, including healings.[11]

Be that as it may, sometimes, in His mercy and in His purposes,
He will heal immediately. But at other times His healing will go on
at a deeper level in the innermost parts of our being and not be fully
realized in our bodies until we step into our new bodies upon our
arrival at our Father's house. And yes, He has redeemed us, but He is
also continuing that redemptive process in our lives right up until we
draw our last breath. Yes, we are healed by His stripes, or wounds, but
we are a work in process, and He isn't finished with us yet!

As Henry Frost said:

Christ did die to destroy sickness, and He will
yet do it. But He does not say that He will, in a
perfect sense, do it now, but rather, at a later time
when He comes in power and great glory.[12]

The fact is, when it comes to the health and strength of our earthly
bodies, He doesn't ask everyone to walk the same path.

When the resurrected Christ told Peter how he was going to die
to glorify the Lord, Peter looked over his shoulder at John and said,
"Lord, what about him?" Jesus patiently replied, "If I want him to
remain alive until I return, what is that to you? You must follow me."[13]
In other words, Jesus has His own purpose for each of us. And whatever situation He gives us in life, we're to follow Him in faith and trust.

God has different purposes for His own, and He shows Himself strong and gains glory in different ways throughout each of our lifetimes. And if He allows suffering in our lives, He does for very specific, very important reasons, and He does not do so lightly!

In the Phillips translation of 2 Corinthians 4:7–10, Paul writes these words:

> This priceless treasure we hold, so to speak, in common earthenware—to show that the splendid power of it belongs to God and not to us. We are hard-pressed on all sides, but we are never frustrated; we are puzzled, but never in despair. We are persecuted, but are never deserted: we may be knocked down but we are never knocked out! Every day we experience something of the death of Jesus, so that we may also show the power of the life of Jesus in these bodies of ours.

Hard-pressed? Puzzled? Persecuted? Knocked down? Yes, yes, and more besides on some days! And just how does His life show up in our bodies? Through death! Through hardship! (That must really get Satan down some days, don't you think?)

Paul says that as believers we're clay pots, common earthenware jars meant to hold priceless treasure through the course of our lives. That impossibly valuable treasure is nothing less than "the light of the knowledge of the glory of God in the face of Christ" (2 Cor. 4:6).

Each of these earthenware jars has been handmade by God Himself, our Creator and the master artisan—not stamped out in some mass-production factory in China. So as with all handmade items, we are unique. No two exactly alike. And if our very life purpose is to display the treasure we contain within, that display often works best when there are faults and cracks and chips in the pot! It is through these that the radiant, resplendent glory of Jesus shines through to the wondering eyes of the world.

Thinking about this same passage, author Robert Jewitt asked the question, "What would carry the same significance in our day as the clay pot of the first century?" The answer he came up with: a cardboard box! Our bodies, to paraphrase 2 Corinthians, are like the box your new shoes came in. Like a Christmas package in a big, cardboard FedEx mailer. But *within* that box, as with Paul's jars of clay, we hold a priceless treasure.

Years ago now, my own dear mother, Lindy Eareckson, left this earth for heaven. In that moment, she had no more need of the box that had wrapped her for eighty-seven years. It was empty, with worn-out corners, bends, and wrinkles. And yet it had been the vessel in which the treasure of the Spirit of Christ had dwelt. We loved that "box" because she was in it—and because she let Jesus shine through it. And He had shone all the more brightly through the edges, tears, and thin places of that box as it began to collapse with age. He was radiant in her, shining mightily as she served our family, as she stuck by my side all the years I was in the hospital, and as she gave and gave and gave.

But now the treasure is safely home, the box discarded and left behind.

The point is that Jesus revealed Himself in my mother in quite a different way than He desires to reveal Himself through me or through you. My box is not your box. My packaging is not your packaging. And I believe with all my heart that sometimes it is through the lives of those who are mentally or physically challenged, or those bearing up under suffering, that Jesus chooses to shine in the most spectacular ways.

Would you take that decision away from our sovereign God as the so-called faith healer I quoted at the beginning of this chapter would?

Would you dictate to Him the kind of box He should use to store His treasure? Would you complain if the box had a few holes in it to better let people see the dazzling wealth inside?

In my last book I wrote about Cindy, a young woman with cerebral palsy who happened to be the last person to participate in a talent night at one of our Joni and Friends family retreats. Cindy's mother pushed her daughter, in her wheelchair, out onto the platform. Cindy, she told us, had been working hard all week on her song, "Amazing Grace."

Several of us looked at each other. We all loved Cindy, but how was this going to work? Because of her disability, Cindy couldn't speak.

Then her mother walked off stage and left Cindy alone. The young woman laboriously stretched out her twisted fingers and pushed a button on her communication device attached to her chair. And out came the monotone computerized voice: *Amazing grace, how sweet the sound, that saved a wretch like me....*

As the robotic voice continued the hymn, Cindy turned her head to face us, the audience, and with enormous effort, mouthed all the words as best she could. What's more, her smile lit up the entire place.

It was a performance that any opera star or recording artist would envy. To be honest, I had never seen anything to equal it—from that day to this. "Amazing Grace" is not a new song, but that night, it was sung in an entirely new way. Although Cindy was unable to sing the words with her vocal chords, something happened as she leaned hard on Jesus and mouthed those words.

I can't explain how, but somehow it rose up in that auditorium as a ringing hymn of praise to God. It was though Cindy's song was backed by an eighty-piece orchestra. I can imagine the angels, filled with wonder, leaning over the edge of heaven to catch every word.

My friend, that's what I'm talking about.

God revealed Himself in a mighty way, gaining great glory through Cindy's song in front of that audience—and all the unseen hosts of heaven. No one else on earth could have done that in just the way Cindy did. Because of her profound weakness, the treasure of Jesus' life shown through in a way that not even the most technically correct performance on *American Idol* could have come close to matching.

Would you tell Cindy that she was "out of the will of God" because of her disability? That her performance was somehow inadequate? I would be careful about ever letting words like that out of my mouth. I have a strong feeling that God took that performance very seriously.

As Henry Frost wrote:

> Christ has many things to think of in planning
> for a saint; He must have in mind what is best
> for the individual; what is the greatest profit in
> respect to His testimony; what is required in his
> relationship to many other saints; and what is to
> make most for God's present and eternal glory;
> and He will hold resolutely, in answering prayer,
> to that course which will combine in bringing
> the largest and most enduring good to pass.[14]

One more illustration comes to mind. I think of a little Down syndrome boy named Isaiah Nicklas. Barely a toddler, he has sparkling eyes and a shock of red hair.

And Isaiah has a powerful ministry.

How could that be, you ask? How could this child have an actual ministry for Jesus? I'll let his older sister, Mary, share exactly what her little brother's ministry is all about. Mary and Isaiah are covenant children; their parents covered them in prayer long before they were ever born. Those children are part of "the household of faith" in the Nicklas family, and from the very beginning, their parents have encouraged them to explore the ministry that God has blessed them with.

Mary was the one who told me—as she was feeding little Isaiah at the table, spooning the food his way—"All of us in our family have a ministry. Just look at Isaiah!"

At that point Isaiah turned and gave me the biggest, happiest grin. At the same time, his eyes sparkled and his cheeks got just like two little apples.

I really don't know how to describe what I saw that day. "Come on, Joni," someone might say. "It was a toddler's smile." I'm just here to tell you there was something that set that smile apart. It was transcendent. It *glowed*. And it gave me so much joy to see him.

"See what I mean?" Mary said. "Isaiah has his own ministry, too. It's his smile!" She was right. The little boy's face beamed with happiness beyond this world. If you ever wanted to see pure joy right out of the heavenly tap, it was there in Isaiah's countenance.

Let's go back to our verse in 2 Corinthians 4:6: "For God, who said, 'Let light shine out of darkness,' made his light shine in our hearts to give us the light of the knowledge of the glory of God in the face of Christ." Even a little child with Down syndrome can have the light of Christ. I might even say *especially* a little child with Down syndrome.

It's all about the glory of God, isn't it? That's what Henry Frost said:

> Let us then not say God cannot heal and will not
> do so. Let us rather say God can heal and will do
> so if it is for His glory.
>
> … The saint is to remember … that God is
> the judge as to whether or not He will display

Himself and His power by a miraculous act,
and also when, where, how, and with whom
this will be done; and he is to keep constantly
in mind that God is just as faithful and loving
when He does not so display Himself as when
He does.[15]

Amen!

4. As with other crucial issues, Satan will seek to push us into nonbiblical extremes on this issue of miraculous healing.

Henry Frost wisely wrote: "It is my impression that often those persons who have considered the subject of miraculous healing have been extremists, opposing it *in toto* or else endorsing it *in toto*, when neither the one nor the other is justifiable."[16]

Extremists! How our adversary loves it when people who claim to speak for God stake out unyielding, brick-hard positions on issues where Scripture allows for more than one viewpoint or interpretation.

Frost went on to say:

Satan, in seeking to destroy the peace and useful-
ness of the children of God, has many methods
of attack, and none is more effective than when
he attempts to lead them in to unbalanced and
extravagant positions.... Any doctrine may easily be distorted; but here is one which ... may
readily be thrown into large disproportion by one

who holds it and enjoys its benefits. And this, it
seems to me, many persons have done and are
doing, and with serious consequences.[17]

To me, there is one thing that seems to be a common element in
those who take extreme positions on divine healing.

A lack of humility.

On the one hand you have people telling God what He *must* do,
and on the other hand you have people telling God what He *can't* do.
I wouldn't want to be in either position. Who am I, that common
earthenware jar we talked about, to dictate terms to the master potter
and tell Him that He *has* to heal me *right now*? Who am I to tell God
what He can or can't do in today's world?

Bottom line: He can do as He likes. *He is God.* As He declares
in the book of Isaiah, "My purpose will stand, and I will do all that I
please" (46:10). As Job asserts, "He stands alone, and who can oppose
him? He does whatever he pleases" (23:13).

I prefer the approach of the leper who came to Jesus, knelt down
in the dirt, and said, "Lord, if you are willing, you can make me clean."
The gospel writer tells us that Jesus reached out His hand and touched
the man, and said, "I am willing.... Be clean!"[18]

Sometimes He *is* willing to heal immediately—and He will perform
a miracle that modern medicine can't begin to explain. I remember so
well a personal friend of mine, a mature Christian woman who suffered
from a severe bone marrow disease. Every known medical procedure
having failed, the doctors gave her a short time to live. But she and others prayed, and when she returned to the doctor for examination, he
dropped his jaw in amazement. The man was not a believer in Christ,
but after taking repeated blood tests over a period of time he told my
friend, "There is no natural or medical explanation I can give. Your
situation was beyond hope. All I can say is that this is a miracle."[19] And

it was no temporary situation. After fifteen years, the woman was still going strong.

At other times, however—and for reasons we can't always fathom—He is *not* willing to heal a particular illness, reverse the course of a disease, or cancel a particular disability. As with the apostle Paul, who had his request for healing denied, the Lord Jesus will give an extra measure of His presence and grace instead.

That's why I have so appreciated the words of Henry Frost through the years. While he firmly believed in the compassion of Christ and in His power to heal and perform miracles among us, his beliefs were always balanced and tempered by a heart of submission to the mysteries of God's sovereign will and purposes.

When I get to heaven, Henry and I are going to sit by some bright, crystal stream in a field of wildflowers and have a long talk. For now, however, I will leave the final word in this chapter to him.

We need to have confidence in the power of God in respect to our mortal frames, being assured that He is greater than we think. Let us lay it to heart that Christ is still a miracle-worker, with as much power as when He went about on earth healing all manner of sickness and all manner of disease (Matt. 4:23).

> *As long as we give Him the ultimate right of choice, and are as submissive and thankful to Him when He says no as when He says yes, we may freely urge our physical claims upon Him, and this with much expectation.* There are many saints who are not well and many others who are not strong, simply because they have never asked God to be their physical sufficiency.[20]

FOUR

WHAT BENEFIT IS THERE TO MY PAIN?

Love is something more stern and
splendid than mere kindness.
—C. S. Lewis, *The Problem of Pain*

My friends who love to hike in the wilderness (and I would be right there with them if I could) tell me that the best trails are ones that "open up" now and then, giving them a wide-angle perspective on where they have been and where they are in relation to their goal.

In other words, it's great to stop at vistas. If you can find a vantage point in life where the horizon fills your vision and you can gain a bit of perspective, you're in a very good place.

A flat rock at a high overlook, warmed by the sun, is a first-rate place for a slightly smunched peanut butter and jam sandwich out of the backpack—or maybe just a swig of cool water.

Some trails wind endlessly through the forest, never emerging from the sheltering canopy of tree boughs. They're nice, too, of course. I can remember walking such wooded trails in Maryland in my early days—especially savoring the autumn afternoons, with the wine-sweet smell of fallen leaves and the crunch of that red and golden carpet under my feet. (The memories are faint, but still there!)

But after a few hours of walking, you begin to want to see some sky. You crave a viewpoint—maybe on a little hill or high rock—where you can cast your eyes back on the winding path behind you, taking a little well-earned satisfaction in your progress.

I think the author of Psalm 119 had found one of those places in his life where he could pause, catch his breath, and take that long view behind him before squaring his shoulders, tightening the straps on his pack, and setting out on the trail once again.

His words remind me again—on a day when I need reminding—that even though pain and suffering may be our experience during our brief earthly passage, our Lord knows how to turn even such disappointments and hardships toward our favor and help. I'd like to capture several of those benefits in the next few pages—and give thanks for them.

Benefit No. 1: Suffering Can Turn Us from a Dangerous Direction

Looking back over his life (if not his hiking trail), the psalmist scribbled these words in his journal:

> Before I was afflicted I went astray,
> but now I obey your word.
> (Ps. 119:67)

"Well," you may say, "I've heard that before. That's really nothing new."

But think about it: For this man at this particular place in his life, it *was* something new. And the thought stopped him in his tracks. It had suddenly dawned on him that the trouble in his life—sorrowful, upsetting, annoying, pressure-packed, or painful as it may have been at the time—had been good for him, and had been specifically allowed by God to benefit him.

Say what you will, my friend, but that is a profound realization for anyone.

No, he wasn't saying that the trouble itself had been good. Far from it! But looking back, he could (now) honestly admit that it had produced a good effect.

It had *turned* him … and he'd needed turning.

He had been heading one direction, then—wham!—he was flattened by this whatever-it-was event in his life.

He frankly acknowledged that before this "affliction" came—an injury, an illness, a financial reversal, a broken love affair, who knows?— he was heading down an unwise, unhealthy path. In the back of his mind, in his heart of hearts, he might have known it was wrong. And yet he couldn't—or wouldn't—turn back. The path he had felt so determined to follow might have taken him into a foolish marriage, a careless business deal, alcoholism, pornography, estrangement from his children, criminal activities, or maybe just into a proud, careless lifestyle that pushed God to the far margins.

Then the affliction came. The bad thing that became a good thing.

The wound. The disappointment. The setback. The pink slip. The rejection. The heartache. The divorce. The failure. The doctor's report.

That intruder in his life—whatever it was—took hold of both his shoulders and wrenched him a little (or a lot), dragging him back on course. And now, many happy miles down the right road, he was looking back and saying to himself, "You know that was a *very* hard thing, but thank God for it! Lord, You are good and do good. I'm so thankful. If I had kept heading in that direction—if I had insisted on going my own way—who knows what would have happened?"

It didn't mean that his troubles all went away. No, the implication in the following verses is that at least some circumstances in his life continued to bring a great deal of pain to his heart. But even as he reflects on these things, the strong assurance once again wells up in his heart:

> It was good for me to be afflicted
> so that I might learn your decrees.
> (v. 71)

Benefit No. 2: Suffering Reminds Us Where Our True Strength Lies

The scenario I just described is *so* God. That whole way of looking at life runs precisely counter to the way most people naturally think or respond.

One of the reasons I *know* the Bible is true is by the way its wisdom runs consistently cross-grain to common human assumptions. God's Word never, ever tags along behind human thinking and philosophies, never tries to stay in style, never seeks to accommodate itself or somehow make itself "relevant."

No, God's truth simply *is*, like a towering mountain, majestic and serene, dominating the horizon, utterly unmoved by wind or weather or the fickle judgments of the so-called opinion makers in our world.

Take the biblical teaching on human strength.

In the pages of Scripture, authentic strength—of the sort that wins battles, overcomes impossible odds, and takes on overwhelming opposition—walks hand in hand with *weakness*.

Now, that's anything but a popular notion. It's definitely not Hollywood. And yet it is true ten thousand times over. Those in Scripture who take pride in their own might or prowess or superior resources fail and fail again. But those who acknowledge their weakness and their need, those who cry out to God in their heartbreak and frustration and utter inability, those whose need for Christ isn't partial, but total, find vast amounts of strength beyond their own.

One of the last words recorded in red in the New Testament, prior to the book of Revelation, are the words of Jesus to the apostle Paul, when He said: "My grace is sufficient for you, *for my power is made perfect in weakness*" (2 Cor. 12:9).

The word *perfect* springs from the same Greek term that Jesus used when He cried out from the cross with His last breath, "It is finished!"

Tetélestai! Accomplished. Done. Fulfilled. Paid in full.

To Paul, in his weakness and distress, Jesus said, *"Teleítai!* My power is accomplished or brought to *completion* in your weakness or frailty."

Ah, but here's the rub. To access that incomparable resurrection power, you and I must first be thoroughly convinced of our own utter bankruptcy and turn to Him with all our hearts. As C. S. Lewis wrote on one occasion, we must "fall into Jesus."

You would think that this simple truth would be a no-brainer for a person like me, in a wheelchair. But it hasn't always been so.

I can't recall how far back it was—maybe when I was at the University of Maryland in the late sixties or early seventies—but I was really big on "being independent" in those early days of my paralysis. I remember wheeling around that huge campus, my face a mask of determination, firmly resolved to "make my own way."

Absurd? Yes. In denial? Probably. Bound to fail? Of course.

Nevertheless, I'd made up my mind that there would be no special considerations or help for me in my classes, and that I would feed myself in the cafeteria using a special spoon inserted into my arm splint. I didn't want to be "treated any differently," although quite obviously my needs and challenges were vastly different from 99 percent of my fellow students.

The truth is, I didn't want anyone to see me as "weak" or "needy."

As a consequence of this mind-set, there was one particular Scripture verse I never wanted anyone to quote in my presence. It was 1 Corinthians 12:23, where Paul says to treat the parts of the body that seem to be weaker with special honor. I looked at that verse as nothing more than a pity-the-poor-unfortunate perspective on people like me in wheelchairs. Treated with *special honor?* No, sir. Not me. I was young and strong. I was on my own. I wasn't weak. I could handle it. Get the picture?

Years later, God's wisdom began to seep into my soul—it takes awhile sometimes, doesn't it?—and I began to see the real truth behind 1 Corinthians 12. It's not a pity-the-poor-disabled verse at all. On the contrary, I think the whole chapter makes the point that we are *all* weak, *all* needy, whether we like to admit it or not. And what is it that we need? We need each other in the body of Christ. It just happens the weaknesses of some people (like me) are more evident.

People who have obvious disabilities more readily get what it means to be weak and feel needy. As a result, maybe the light goes on a little sooner for us when we hear the apostle Paul say, "I will boast all the more gladly about my weaknesses, so that Christ's power may rest on me.... For when I am weak, then I am strong" (2 Cor. 12:9,10).

There's that theme again: strength out of weakness. Profound life direction growing right out of seemingly immovable obstacles in our path.

I think back to my high school friend Bobby who never took God seriously until trouble hit. Bagging a football scholarship to a Big Ten university consumed all his attention. But during his sophomore year he got slammed down hard on the five-yard line. Two surgeries and three sidelined seasons later, he had done some serious thinking. Life was short. Where were his priorities?

Today, he's still into sports. (He coaches the Tiny Tornadoes after work.) But his priorities are straighter. Bible study and prayer get their chunk of time on his schedule now, and I don't think that would have happened—*Bobby* doesn't think it would have happened—had it not been for that painful moment of destiny on the five-yard line.

Then look what happened to my neighbors who used to live down the street. When the Southern California economy was flying high, Brian and his family had all the materialistic toys and status symbols their hearts desired. But then the state's economy tanked. Brian lost his job and found himself with some serious thinking to do.

In fact, the family will tell you now that it was one of the best things that could have happened to them. They discovered that God was still on the throne, cared deeply about the direction of their lives, and was fully able to care for them as they climbed back on their feet. They also found that family meant more than possessions, and that community college wasn't so bad for their college-bound daughter, who had her heart set on Princeton. I don't think my neighbors would have learned all that had it not been for Brian's losing his job.

Remember the psalmist's words? "It was *good* for me to be afflicted, so that I might learn your decrees."

And finally, I'm thinking of my twenty-six-year-old cousin whose girl-friend returned the engagement ring. He let it sit on his dresser for months as a monument to his failed love life. Finally, he dealt with his grief by pouring himself into a troubled kid who lived two doors down and had never known a father. He took him to the stables on weekends and taught him to ride horseback. It made the jilted young man grow up. He learned that his problems, which had at first loomed so large in his eyes, were really pretty small potatoes after all.

Two years later, my cousin ducked into a bookstore to buy a present and spied a honey-blonde girl with a knock-out smile flipping through a calendar of palomino horses. They got to talking and discovered they had more in common than just equines. He took her riding the next weekend, joined the singles group at her church, and not long afterward, she said a big yes when he popped the question on her front-porch swing. Today he shudders to think that he could have missed her. And frankly, it just wouldn't have all panned out that way had he never felt the crush of being rejected by his first girlfriend.

Who can understand the ways of God? As Solomon noted, "A man's steps are directed by the LORD. How then can anyone understand his own way?" (Prov. 20:24). The truth is that you and I—if we see anything at all—perceive only the dimmest outline or shadow of God's plan and purpose. His ways are often mysterious, and it's beyond our capacity to analyze His actions or predict what He might do next.

As the prophet Isaiah asked:

> Who has understood the mind of the LORD,
> Or instructed him as his counselor?[1]

The answer: no one. Not ever.

But even with our limited understanding, with time and with much prayer, the daylight dawns, and we discover what Jeremiah told us so many centuries ago: God's plans for us really are full of hope and a future.

Even when that path leads through pain.

Benefit No. 3: Suffering Restores a Lost Beauty in Christ

Maybe, like me, you've occasionally worried that the cares, troubles, and afflictions of life will simply begin to wear you down, dulling your joy, diluting your hope, and robbing you of the radiance you once experienced as a believer.

In fact, it may be the very opposite.

It isn't the hurts, blows, and bruises that rob us of the freshness of Christ's beauty in our lives. More likely, it is careless ease, empty pride, earthly preoccupations, and too much prosperity that will put layers of dirty film over our souls.

I'll never forget years ago when I had a chance to visit Notre Dame Cathedral while I was in Paris. There it was, almost one thousand years old, standing there so huge and ... black. I had never seen such a dirty cathedral! After hundreds of years of soot, dust, and smoke, Notre Dame was covered in layers of black grime. It was even difficult to make out the beautiful carvings and details on the exterior.

But then the grand old cathedral went through a years-long restoration. Scaffolding was erected, and the entire exterior was sandblasted. I was stunned when I saw a recent photograph of the cathedral. It was beautiful—and so very different from the way I remembered it. I wonder if the people who have lived under its great shadow for many years recognized it.

The ancient stones glowed bright and golden. You could see details on carvings that hadn't been visible in decades. It was like a different cathedral. What a wonder a bit of strategic sandblasting can accomplish!

When I use the word *sandblasting*—and when I think of how that process changed that cathedral in Paris—I can't help but consider the way God uses suffering to sandblast you and me. There's nothing like real hardships to strip off the veneer in which you and I so carefully cloak ourselves. Heartache and physical pain reach below the superficial, surface places of our lives, stripping away years of accumulated indifference and neglect. When pain and problems press us up against a holy God, suffering can't help but strip away years of dirt. Affliction has a way of jackhammering our character, shaking us up and loosening our grip on everything we hold tightly.

But the beauty of being stripped down to the basics, sandblasted until we reach a place where we feel empty and helpless, is that God can fill us up with Himself. When pride and pettiness have been removed, God can fill us with "Christ in you, the hope of glory."

Suffering doesn't teach you about yourself from a textbook—it teaches you from experience. It empties you so that by faith you can be filled with His Spirit.

Where's the benefit? The process of divine sandblasting can reveal something quite beautiful—not only on the outside, but on the inside. And people may find themselves seeing something in you—some grace or quality of life—they had never seen before, or hadn't seen for years and years.

It was Nathaniel Hawthorne who said, "Christian faith is a grand cathedral with divinely pictured windows. Standing without you see no glory" (Maybe, like me, you see a rather dark and dirty cathedral.) "But standing within, every ray of light reveals a harmony of unspeakable splendors."[2]

Let affliction have its perfect work. The result?

Nothing short of the unspeakable splendor of Christ in you, the hope of glory.

Benefit No. 4: Suffering Can Heighten Our Thirst for Christ

I can remember a strenuous backpacking trip through the Rawah Wilderness of northern Colorado. Even though that trip was long ago, before the accident that ended my hiking career, I recall that adventure as if it were yesterday.... Ah, that burning, aching feeling in my legs as we hiked up steep mountains, the feel of the hot, high-mountain sun on my face. Most of all, I remember dipping my canteen into the Cache la Poudre River after a long, tiring morning on the trail.

It's not that I *needed* to fill my canteen just then. In fact, it was already mostly full. But after hours in the hot sun, the water was warm, metallic, and tasted a little bit stale. Why drink *that* when there was a rushing mountain river of fresh, crystal-clear, ice-cold water right at my feet? No way was I going to sip tepid tap water from my canteen! When you've got the real deal, why waste your thirst on second best?

I thought of that morning by the Cache la Poudre when I recently read a special verse in the book of Jeremiah. God tells the prophet, "My people have committed two sins: They have forsaken me, the spring of living water, and have dug their own cisterns, broken cisterns that cannot hold water."[3]

Now that little canteen of mine, metallic and warm as it may have been, could definitely hold water, but I think you get the point. So many of us settle for second-best things that really cannot and do not satisfy.

And here's the jarring thing: God calls that sin.

It is an offense to Him when we Christians know full well that Jesus is the clear, fresh, and satisfying Living Water ... and yet we turn to the attractions of this world, telling ourselves that such substitute pleasures truly can and do refresh and satisfy.

Where are our heads? When we choose earthly things over godly things, it's like, well, licking the inside of a hot, empty, leaky canteen, and saying, "Oh yes, more, more! This tastes so great. This is *so* refreshing!" Really, we're not even convincing ourselves. Yet we try to do so time and again.

Jesus is *the* spring of Living Water, and when we drink of Him, out of us flow *rivers* of living water. And the offense against God comes when we know that Jesus is the only one who satisfies, yet still dig around in the dust and sand, groping for cisterns that can't hold half a teacup of tepid tap water.

That's where the offense against God comes, when we in effect tell Him that Jesus doesn't satisfy. That He's not enough. That He doesn't refresh. That we need something else—something more. Something better.

This is the point, I believe, at which God sometimes allows His discipline to enter our lives. Sometimes we become so enamored with our tinny, brackish canteen water that we can't even see the rushing crystal stream at our very feet. We forget all about it. But then when trials or suffering overwhelm our lives, it dawns on us that all of our God-substitutes fall pitifully short of helping us.

Thirsty, dry, and weary beyond telling, we finally push aside our leaky canteens and fall on our knees beside the Never-Failing Stream. We come back to the fountain. And when we do, we sometimes realize that if God hadn't allowed the hurt or suffering in our lives, we might have wandered for *years,* subsisting on stale, rationed canteen water rather than plunging our faces into the very essence of refreshment and life.

If we allow it, suffering will lead us to the bank of the stream, where we can always find a long, cold drink of the refreshing grace of the Lord Jesus.

Benefit No. 5: Suffering Can Increase Our Fruitfulness

As I look out my window now, I'm noticing the early blossoms on some of the fruit trees—a sight that never fails to touch my heart, bringing back a poignant childhood memory.

Around this time of year our family used to pack our bags and head up to western Maryland near the little town of Hancock, where my Uncle Don and Aunt Emma lived. They had a small apple farm, their house nestled on top of a ridge with the orchard spread out below like a wide skirt. In early spring there was row after row of trees laden with fragrant white blossoms. You could stand on the back porch and smell the perfume, hear the drone of busy bees.

It was a truly beautiful orchard, and I hope it's still there. But even if it's been leveled to make room for a big-box store or a subdivision, it shines in my memory. And it also holds a deep secret about God.

You see, early spring is grafting time. Uncle Don would select his trees, find just the right place on the bark, peel it away, and make a slanting cut into the heart of the wood. He would then take a small branch, whittle its end, then push the graft into the damp center of the tree, covering the union to keep it cool and moist. Later that spring, new life would emerge: blossoms to tiny buds to beautiful fruit.

But it didn't happen without a wounding in both the tree and branch.

If you could interview the tree at the time of the surgery, I suspect it wouldn't be all that happy about the prospect of being cut to the core and accepting this alien graft into its very flesh. But late in the summer, when the enhanced, abundant fruit hangs heavy on the new limb ... well, at that point the tree might be willing to amend its opinion.

John Bunyan once wrote:

> Conversion is not the smooth, easy-going process
> some men seem to think. It is wounding work, of
> course, this breaking of the hearts, but without
> wounding there is no saving.... Where there is
> grafting there is a cutting, the scion must be let in
> with a wound; to stick it onto the outside or tie it
> on with a string would be of no use. Heart must
> be set to heart and back to back, or there will be
> no sap from root to branch, and this I say, must
> be done by a wound.[4]

Never would I have dreamed, wandering through that orchard as a child, that my conversion process would be as hard as it has been. I was to learn through my broken neck that there was no saving grace, no saving work apart from a wounding. Yes, wounding of Christ on His cross, but also a wounding when you and I suffer and, as a result, are set, let in, cut into the body of Christ through affliction and hardship. "We must go through many hardships to enter the kingdom of God," it says in the Bible (Acts 14:22).

My Christian life became a wounding work and remains so during this current crisis of chronic pain. My heart has been set to God's like a grafting cut into the living heart of an apple tree. Whether I like it or not, it has been heart to heart and back to back, with so much doubt and fear, heartache and tears. It has definitely not been a smooth, easy-going process—and to this day, it isn't.

Jesus speaks about grafting in John 15:5. It is here He tells His disciples—and you and me, "I am the vine; you are the branches. If a man remains in me and I in him, he will bear much fruit; apart from me you can do nothing."

Friend, you may be going through a time of wounding right now and, if you are, take heart, because your heart is being set to God's, and there is no saving work apart from pain. Your life will produce so much more fruit from it all—fruit that you probably won't even see or know about.

For those whom God loves, He grafts.

Just remember what I have learned these many years: Apart from Him, you can do nothing. But *in Him*, with His life sap flowing through your branch and leaves, you have strength for everything. He said so.

And somehow, the result of all that cutting and wounding, grafting, and healing will be fruit beyond what you have ever produced.

Do We Really Believe This?

Maybe it all comes down to this.

Do we really believe what we say we really believe?

Do we believe that this life is just a brief staging area before real life begins on the other side, in heaven with Jesus? Are we truly counting on the fact that though these physical bodies of ours may change, or become incapacitated or severely limited, our authentic life—hidden with Christ Himself—will continue to grow and blossom and bear fruit through the rest of our years—and then forever beyond that?

In 2 Corinthians 4:16, Paul tells us, "Therefore we do not lose heart. Though outwardly we are wasting away, yet inwardly we are being renewed day by day."

To me, that verse is so comforting. We all know what it feels like to be outwardly wasting away because we see it happening every time we look in a mirror. But I have a friend for whom that verse isn't only a great comfort, it's life itself.

Melinda is struggling with a severe—and I mean heartbreakingly severe—case of diabetes. In the process, she has lost both her legs through amputation. She has lost her eyesight. And she has lost several fingers. Not long ago she called to tell me that the doctors were about to remove another finger. My heart went out to her, as it always does. But my heart is also inspired by her struggle.

And here's why.

Melinda has not lost heart.

The diabetes may be taking much away from her, but it can't take *that* away. The doctors can't amputate *that*. The woman is quite literally wasting away, week by week, day by day. But she has not lost heart because she places her trust and confidence in Christ. Melinda knows that no one—no disease—can take away the real Melinda, because He is actually renewing her day by day.

In some ways, I am convinced she's getting even stronger. Why? How? Precisely *because* she is getting weaker! The more physical ability Melinda loses, the more she leans on Christ. And the harder she leans on Christ, the stronger she becomes.

Again, do we truly believe that? Do we believe that what Jesus told Paul was literally true—that His power is made perfect in weakness? I do. And I believe it for Melinda. Although I can't explain it, I know that somehow, some way, the power of God's Son, the mighty Creator and Redeemer of the world, is being perfected in this young woman's life.

Her grafting to Jesus, through many wounds, is profound beyond telling.

You and I may not see it with our physical eyes, but it is being seen ... by the hosts of heaven and hell, and perhaps by those saints who have gone before her who fill the heavenly grandstands and cheer her on in the race of her life. Who knows what the eternal results of her courage and faithfulness will mean? Dare we even speculate?

You may not have a debilitating disease like dear Melinda, but you do know—all of us do—what it means to be outwardly wasting away day by day. Perhaps you find yourself in your late fifties now, and the changes are encroaching; your limitations—the aches and pains—are catching you by surprise. Well, these are all little wake-up calls, as far as I'm concerned. Little alarm clocks, little waving yellow flags, small signals that remind us that as we are wasting away, we can go to God in our weakness to be renewed and made stronger day by day.

And what does the rest of Melinda's favorite verse say?

> For our light and momentary troubles are achieving for us an eternal glory that far outweighs them all. So we fix our eyes not on what is seen, but on what is unseen. For what is seen is temporary, but what is unseen is eternal. (2 Cor. 4:17–18)

Feet and toes, hands and fingers, wonderful as they may be, are only temporary appendages to help us get around in this temporary world. But the soul is eternal. That alone is worth all the "light and momentary troubles."

Just ask Melinda.

FIVE

HOW CAN I GO ON LIKE THIS?

We say, then, to anyone who is under trial, give
Him time to steep the soul in His eternal truth.
Go into the open air, look up into the depths of
the sky, or out upon the wideness of the sea, or
on the strength of the hills that is His also; or, if
bound in the body, go forth in the spirit; spirit
is not bound. Give Him time and, as surely as
dawn follows night, there will break upon the
heart a sense of certainty that cannot be shaken.

—Amy Carmichael

In the dark, in the night, after two in the morning when the pain medication has worn off and sleep has fled, I have faced the stark reality of my life as it is, and asked myself, *How can I go on like this?*

How can I endure another sleepless night?

How can I go through another morning routine of just trying to get a pain-wracked, uncooperative body ready for the day?

How can I keep my commitments, lead by example, discharge my responsibilities at Joni and Friends, and hold onto my joy when this vise of pain keeps crushing me tighter and tighter?

Such questions will come, of course.

With David, I sometimes sigh, "How long must I wrestle with my thoughts and every day have sorrow in my hear? How long will my enemy triumph over me?"[1]

It's all right to ask the questions, and certainly God is neither put off nor offended by our anguished, middle-of-the-night queries. But there is also a time to set the questions aside and think again about answers—good, satisfying answers—He has already given to me through the years.

Answer No. 1: I Can Go On ... Because God Moves through Time with Me.

On a hot, sultry July afternoon five years ago, Ken and I observed the thirty-eighth anniversary of a very similar afternoon in 1967 when I broke my neck. In fact, we invited a couple of friends up to our house to celebrate with a dinner of my mother's famous crab cakes.

Celebrate, you say?

The dictionary defines the word as observing a day or commemorating an event with ceremonies or festivities. Honestly, I can't think of a better word, given all the good things that have happened as a result of my wheelchair. This particular anniversary marked exactly thirty-eight years since that fateful day of my injury, and we commemorated it with ... crabs.

And why not?

We all knew I'd be dead were it not for that feisty Chesapeake Bay blue crab that bit my sister in the water. When that little crustacean snapped at her toe, she whirled around and screamed to me, "Joni, watch out for crabs!" Kathy had no idea I had just dived off the raft. She didn't know my head had struck a sandbar, cracking my neck—and that I was floating face down, holding my breath, and desperately hoping she'd see me, that she'd come and rescue me!

Thankfully, God got her attention with a crab, and when Kathy couldn't see me, she became alarmed. That's when she caught sight of my blonde hair floating on the water's surface. "Joni!" she yelled. "Joni! Are you okay?!" Little did she know I was within seconds of drowning.

She swam to me in the nick of time. As Kathy hoisted me out of the water, I sputtered and gasped for oxygen. When I saw my arm slung over her shoulder—yet couldn't feel it—I became nauseous. I knew something terrible had happened.

From that instant, life would never be the same.

And it was so long ago.

Later, after we finished dinner, we took a minute to close out the anniversary dinner with a short reading from John 5.

> Now there is in Jerusalem near the Sheep Gate a pool, which in Aramaic is called Bethesda and which is surrounded by five covered colonnades. Here a great number of disabled people used to lie—the blind, the lame, the paralyzed. One who was there had been an invalid for thirty-eight years. When Jesus saw him lying there and learned that he had been in this condition for a long time, he asked him, "Do you want to get well?" (John 5:2–6)

At that point we stopped. "Look at that," I said, smiling. "Here it is, my thirty-eighth anniversary of quadriplegia, and it actually states that Jesus thought thirty-eight years of paralysis was *a long time.*"

What an anniversary present! The Lord of the universe who lives outside the confines of time, the Alpha and Omega, the Beginning and the

End, who existed before time began—this Jesus feels that living without the use of your legs for thirty-eight years is a *long* time.

"I'm glad for that," I said, shaking my head, "because *I* sure think it's a long time."

There have been occasions, I will admit, when I wondered if God empathized—I mean *really* understood—how I felt, how I have groaned in my paralyzed body and hurt as each year brought more aches and pains. I have wondered because of verses like 1 Peter 5:10, which says, "And the God of all grace … *after you have suffered a little while,* will himself restore you and make you strong, firm and steadfast." I like the part about being made strong, but the passage seems to imply that thirty-eight years of suffering is considered only "a little while." In other words, the Bible makes it sound as if those years of anguish are but a blink of an eye. Doesn't God *know* how interminable that much time can feel in a wheelchair? Isn't He aware of how endless a sleepless night, shot through with searing pain, can seem? What kind of wristwatch is He wearing?!

In fact, He does know. He is aware. And for me, the sweet passage in the gospel of John lays the issue to rest. When Jesus saw the paralyzed man lying on the straw mat by the Pool of Bethesda, we can picture His eyes welling with tears. He saw more than a lonely, disabled man waiting—without any real hope—by the waters rumored to heal. We can imagine Jesus kneeling down to gently touch him. The Savior's heart went out to that poor soul whose legs were withered and useless. It's no mistake that Holy Writ says that God thinks thirty-eight years of paralysis is a long haul.

How could that be? First of all, Scripture reminds us that "He Himself knows our frame; He is mindful that we are but dust" (Ps. 103:14 NASB). But beyond the declaration of intimate knowledge regarding that fragile, earthly tent that houses our eternal soul, God went infinitely further to identify with our frailties. As a result, He who was ever beyond time decided before time to *enter* time, experiencing the passing hours and days and years with those He created. He didn't have to, but He did. And I believe His Holy Spirit "experiences" life with us moment-by-moment, day by day, turn by turn, mile by mile. He is pleased when we obey Him (even though He already knew we would), and He is truly grieved when we disobey (even though He knew it from the foundation of the earth). He is undoubtedly *with* us, sharing our joys and sorrows, counting our tears, and whispering reminders of His presence.

"Have you forgotten," some might reply, "just whom you're talking about here? Jesus is the Ancient of Days who scattered the galaxies across the heavens and laid the very foundations of the earth. What would thirty-eight years be to Him? Less than a heartbeat!"

Yes, in the sense of Christ's eternity, *any* amount of earthly time is less than a single tick of the clock. For that matter, the whole history of earth is like a day that has gone by, like a watch in the night (Ps. 90).

In our Lord's humanity, however, thirty-eight years was more than His whole lifetime. He knows time in a personal, experiential way. As the writer of Hebrews said, "We don't have a priest who is out of touch with our reality."[2]

The God who created time understands time in all its dimensions.

Even before Jesus walked the earth, when the prophet Jeremiah was placed into a lonely dungeon under the house of Jonathan the secretary, we're told that he remained there "a long time" (Jer. 37:16). How long? A week? A month? Six months? A year? The Bible doesn't say. But for the distraught prophet, the time in that hateful place must have seemed interminable. When King Zedekiah finally pulled him out for a consultation, the prophet begged, "Do not send me back to the house of Jonathan the secretary, or I will die there."[3]

In John 14:9, just before He went to the cross, Jesus said to Philip, "Don't you know me, Philip, *even after I have been among you such a long time?* Anyone who has seen me has seen the Father. How can you say, 'Show us the Father'?"

How long a time? Maybe three to three and a half years? Was that such a lengthy interval? Jesus thought so. It certainly was a long enough period of time for Philip and the other disciples to have understood this most basic, elemental fact about their Lord's identity. In fact, the word Jesus uses here for "a long time" could be translated "a time as vast as this."

When He and His disciples walked a hundred miles from Capernaum to Jerusalem, it was a *long* walk, and it took a long time. And when He was on the cross for six hours, they were six very, very long hours. Six minutes would have been long.

A fistful of years have passed since that crab-cake anniversary dinner. I've now crested more than forty years in my wheelchair, and my bones are thinner and more fragile than ever. In the Bible, the number forty usually means a time of testing. Like the forty days it rained on Noah's ark, or Jesus' being tested in the wilderness for forty days, or the Israelites' wandering in the desert for forty years.

What does God think about four decades of paralysis? I got my answer not long ago when I read Joshua 24:7, where the Lord recounts for His children all the trials they endured after they left Egypt. He tenderly reminds them, "Then you lived in the desert *for a long time.*"

Keep adding the years, and God's loving-kindness only increases in equal measure. Maybe that's why Isaiah 43:18–19 says, "Forget the former things; do not dwell on the past. See, I am doing a new thing!"

I don't know if I'll ever see a miraculous healing this side of my gravestone. But I do know that usually after forty years of testing, after the forty-year trial, there are always moments of victory, power, and jubilation. It's been ages since a Maryland crab and a broken neck began the unfolding of God's plan for me and for the ministry I lead to reach other disabled people with God's loving–kindness. All I know is each ensuing year brings more people with disabilities into the fellowship of sharing in Christ's sufferings. More people who desire to live to the glory of God.

More people whose miracle is a heaven-sent smile, not in spite of the paralysis, but because of it.

I can't begin to describe to you how important these biblical reassurances about time have been to me in my recent battles with nonstop pain. If I thought that I had a God who set aside the business of eternity from time to time to simply check in on me every few years, I don't know how I'd survive.

When you find yourself in chronic agony, life gets reduced to hours rather than days—and sometimes minutes and seconds. When I am in physical distress in the night, unable to sleep, unable to move, and unwilling to awaken Ken (again) to turn me, I need to know that God's concern and care for me is literally breath by breath, heartbeat by heartbeat, moment by moment.

With David, I acknowledge the Lord's sharp attention to my physical and emotional needs.

> I am bowed down and brought very low;
>> all day long I go about mourning.
> My back is filled with searing pain;
>> there is no health in my body.
> I am feeble and utterly crushed;
>> I groan in anguish of heart.
> All my longings lie open before you, O Lord;
>> my sighing is not hidden from you.
> (Ps. 38:6–9)

And also with David, I celebrate the Lord's constant, attentive presence:

> How precious are your thoughts about me, O
>> God!
> They cannot be numbered!

> I can't even count them;
>
> > they outnumber the grains of sand!
>
> (Ps. 139:17–18 NLT)

There's a word picture for you. Visualize all of the sand from every dune, every desert, and every beach in the whole world pouring in a golden torrent—on and on and on, heaping up higher and higher—into the clouds! Those are God's thoughts toward each of His children—outnumbering the grains of sand. The flow of wise, loving, concerned, attentive, watchful, impassioned, infinitely caring thoughts surge on and on, all day, all night, for as long as you live, and forever beyond that. God has infinitely more thoughts about you than there are seconds in your day.

That's a thought that keeps me going. That's a truth that enables me to go on when it seems beyond my ability to do so. And here's another.

Answer No. 2: I Can Go On ... Because I Know God Can Use Broken Instruments to Make Incomparable Music.

Jack Reimer, a syndicated columnist, wrote a story about the great violinist Yitzhak Perlman. Perlman had polio as a child and walks with crutches and braces on both legs. Instead of arranging to be seated on stage at the beginning of his performance, he chooses to walk across the stage methodically and slowly until he reaches his chair. Then he sits down, puts his crutches on the floor, undoes the clasps on his legs, bends down, picks up the violin, nods to the conductor, and proceeds to play. As Reimer describes it, there is a certain majesty in this ritual.

During a 1995 concert, a string on Perlman's violin suddenly snapped, and everyone in the audience could hear it. The great virtuoso stopped and gazed at the broken string as those in attendance that night wondered what he would do. Perlman closed his eyes, and after a moment of reflection, signaled the conductor to begin again.

Though anyone who knows music understands that it's impossible to play a symphonic work with just three stings, Perlman was undaunted. Apparently you could see this superb artist actually recomposing the piece in his head as he went along, inventing new fingering positions to coax never-before-heard sounds from his three-string violin.

The sophisticated New York audience watched and listened in awe, knowing they were witnessing a truly groundbreaking performance. When the piece was over, they exploded into appreciative applause. Mr. Perlman smiled, wiped the sweat from his brow, and said in a soft, reverent tone, "You know, sometimes it is the artist's task to find out how much music you can still make with what you have left."

That's another truth that enables me to keep going. Whatever strings are broken in our lives— if we concentrate, if we apply what we know—we can still play beautiful music with what we have left. In fact, it will be music that no one else can play in the same way.

This is a lesson I've learned in a wheelchair for so many years—and have had to relearn in these days (and nights) of unremitting pain. Sometimes you have to take what's left and coax out of life something new and different. Life becomes a recomposition, a series of new chords.

If you'll accept the analogy, severely disabled people aren't your regular violins, and God doesn't perform in our lives in the ordinary way.

People suffering from debilitating injuries, terminal illnesses, or chronic physical distress aren't your standard musical instruments in the orchestra. We can't do everything able-bodied people can do in their physical strength and mobility and vitality. It takes a special skill to bring music out of a broken instrument, and the one who does deserves recognition and glory.

God is that one.

God is the one who finds incomparable beauty and makes matchless music using the most unexpected and unlikely of instruments. He is the one who told Paul, struggling and agonizing over a nettlesome physical infirmity, "My grace is enough; it's all you need. My strength comes into its own in your weakness."[4]

And in the same way, His melody—His incomparable, heavenly, impossibly beautiful music—somehow comes into its own when it emanates from a broken, battered, but fully yielded human vessel.

It's music that can only come from particular instruments, broken in particular ways, and yielded with particular humility. I also believe it brings God glory in a way that is completely unique on earth or in the heavens. And that's a thought that keeps me going, too.

Music played in the dark may have more spiritual power than music performed in the safe and pleasing light of a daylight concert or a well-lighted concert hall.

A few years ago I remember sitting on the stage at a large pastors' conference in the Philippines. I was so excited to be in such an exotic place, especially during the monsoon season. And sure enough, outside a heavy monsoon rain was falling while the crowd, inside the large hall, was being entertained by a small band of Filipino musicians. Their music was intricate and lively, and the audience was enthralled with their performance.

Suddenly a loud crash of thunder shook the hall, and in the next instant, the entire conference hall was plunged into darkness. The powerful storm had caused the lights to go out. But nobody had bothered to explain that to the *blind* musical troupe! Unfazed in the pitch-blackness of the hall, the musicians played on without skipping a beat.

When their song was over, the audience burst into thunderous applause. The darkness gave us all a unique and amazing appreciation for the extraordinary talent God had given these blind musicians. But what really turned up the wattage on the praise that night was the fact that these artists *played through the dark*.

The same is true when we live for God. Sure, our lives resound with praise when He lights our path and we follow Him. After all, a disciple *should* follow his master. But when there's no light for your path and you follow Him through dark times, the volume and the intensity of praise to God goes up many more decibels.

An unknown psalmist named Ethan the Ezrahite, in a time of apparent national darkness, wrote these words: "Blessed are those who have learned to acclaim you, who walk in the light of your presence, O LORD … for you are their glory and strength."[5]

In other words, when there is no light by which to read the music, those who know their God by heart play on.

And the music changes the darkness itself, creating within it a habitation of praise.

Answer No. 3: I Can Go On … Because Jesus Is My Consolation.

I was feeling pretty down last Sunday afternoon because I'd had to stay in bed and missed church. Pain does that to me every once in awhile, but this time, it made me feel low. Very low.

I was lying on my side with my laptop next to me. Knowing that I could control my computer with voice commands, I opened my Bible software program to look up a few Scriptures.

Up came one of those pop-up pages—a reading from one of Charles Spurgeon's devotionals. I usually click those devotions closed and move on to my Bible study. But this one was on the consoling work of the Holy Spirit. In need of encouragement as I was, I sensed the Spirit whispering, *Go ahead, read about Me!* So that's what I did … and I'm so happy I made that choice. It was all about the work of God's Spirit, described as only Spurgeon can.

He said, "Jesus cheers us."

Those three little words caught my eye. He cheers us not by His physical presence, but through the Holy Spirit. Yes, the Spirit's role is to convict and convince us of sin, to illuminate and instruct our hearts. But His main work is to make glad our tired hearts, to uplift and confirm the weak, to encourage and raise up the downcast, and to comfort us. And He does this all through Christ.

Yes, the Holy Spirit consoles, but Jesus is the consolation. The Holy Spirit may act as a physician, but Christ is the medicine. The Spirit heals, but He does so by applying the balm of Gilead: the Lord Jesus. One might be the Comforter, but the other is true comfort. The Spirit focuses not on His own things, but the things of Christ. Spurgeon reminded me that with such rich provision, why should I be sad or despondent? The Holy Spirit is graciously engaged to be my Comforter. He comes alongside me to show me Christ as I might not see Him when times are happy or when life's smooth and easy.

And surely the Holy Spirit takes His sacred trust seriously. It's the Spirit's greatest joy and pleasure—it's His specific command—to honor Christ by helping you and me. Would the Holy Spirit neglect or ignore the Father's command to encourage us? I don't think so! It's the Spirit's task to strengthen you, and He's one who would never neglect His loving office. He lives within your heart to *make* your heart sturdy and glad, and to remind you of sure and certain promises.

And the beautiful promises that made my heart strong on that Sunday afternoon was Isaiah 61, where it is said of Jesus, "He has come to bind up the wounds of the brokenhearted and to comfort all who mourn ... to bestow on them a crown of beauty instead of mourning, and a garment of praise instead of a spirit of despair."[6]

By the time the afternoon drifted into the evening, I was, well, a different person. I was still in pain and still in bed, but I was at *peace*.

The question with which I've entitled this chapter, "How can I go on like this?" falls directly into the Holy Spirit's mission in your life, and He takes it very seriously. He's already on the job. He's engaged. And if you listen, He will speak the comforting words of Jesus into the deep places of your soul.

Answer No. 4: I Can Go On ... Because Right Now Counts Forever.

I remember when this thought hit me with the greatest force. It was years ago when Ken and I made one of our last visits to my mother, when she still lived on the farm in Maryland. I remember being almost shocked by her appearance. At eighty-seven, she seemed to me but a shadow—a frail, thin shadow—of the strong, athletic woman I remember growing up. I had known she was losing ground, both physically and mentally, but on that trip it hit me with a finality that really took me aback.

She was nervous in our family gatherings and couldn't remember the words of well-loved songs and favorite hymns. I remember watching her trying to talk to my aunt, and when she couldn't find the words, she seemed so bewildered, almost lost.

She is now on the other side with Jesus and my dad, enjoying the wonder of a new, forever-young body and praising God with effortless, endless expressions of joy. But during those days in Maryland on that last visit, her frailty hit me broadside with the awesome fact of my own mortality. I looked at her and it was like the thought had dawned on me for the first time: *That's where I'm heading ... where we're all heading.*

That sobering thought alone was enough to remind me of the stakes involved in life. To be confronted with suffering, whether observing it in another or struggling against it with your own aches and pains ... to be confronted with affliction is a reminder that something immense and cosmic is at stake: a heaven to be reached, a hell to be avoided, and a life on earth to be lived seriously and circumspectly.

Our souls are the battleground on which massive spiritual battles are right now—*right this minute*—being waged. And the stakes are enormous. Beyond our conception.

Here on earth, we're being observed by both the sons and daughters of God (who need an example of how to face suffering) and by those who have not yet bowed their knee to the Lordship of Jesus (who need to see how believers respond to the multifaceted circumstances of life). And beyond these earthly eyes, there are other eyes in the spirit realm—both angelic and demonic—who observe and take note whether or not we trust our God in the crucible of trials and affliction. (Remember Job?) And those who have gone on before us—are they watching too? Some interpret Hebrews 12:1 to mean that there literally are saints seated in heavenly grandstands, observing our battles and cheering us on to triumphs of faith.

There is yet another reason why right now counts for eternity.

The New Testament brims over with the promise of everlasting rewards for those who remain faithful to their calling, even in the face of great suffering. To the suffering believers in Smyrna, Jesus said: "Do not be afraid of what you are about to suffer…. Be faithful, even to the point of death, and I will give you the crown of life" (Rev. 2:10).

Every day of our short lives—even every hour—has eternal consequences for good or ill. Eternity—and the way we'll live in it—is somehow being shaped by our moment-by-moment responses to the life we have before us to live right now.

And so it is only fitting that God should give us some sense of the stakes involved. I'm so grateful that life for us is not an easy road. If it were, if the Lord did not occasionally give us a taste of hell's splashover, you and I would soon forget that this world is not our home. I'm also grateful that He opens our eyes from time to time to the magnitude of this spiritual war we are in. He does this by giving us wonderful foretastes of glory divine in the joys we experience, and He does it by allowing us foretastes of hell in our suffering.

Whatever we are experiencing today, we can be reminded of the eternal stakes involved.

That, too, keeps me going.

It's not easy "going on" right now in my life—but I must go on and I *will* go on, until He calls me home. And for however many more days He gives me to live for Him on this side of heaven, every one of them counts forever.

Three Turns of the Ramp

Five different friends, on five different mornings, drive me from home to work. It means four stoplights, a sharp turn onto the 101, exit, then another three lights, and a right-hand turn onto Agoura Road. There's one more light before you turn onto Ladyface Court, which winds up the hill to the International Disability Center—but I don't count that one, because there's enough room to brake long and slow up to the light.

I know every bend, every intersection of the route. I know it because each stop and turn causes a sharp jag in my back. It's why on the freeway I always ask the girls, "Could we please get out of the slow lane? The trucks have sure made it bumpy."

I may not love the drive to work, but I do love arriving.

Our receptionist recently called it "a little bit of heaven." And so it is. The center stands tall and large, reminding me of the vision that brings me here every day: *to communicate the gospel and to equip Christ-honoring churches worldwide to evangelize and disciple people affected by disability.*

Just this morning as Sandy was driving me up Ladyface, I said with a sigh and a smile, "How many people get to do something each day that literally changes lives for eternity?!"

"We do," she said with a smile into the rearview mirror.

I hit the handicap access plate by the center's front doors, which slowly swing open, and in I wheel—heading not for the elevator, but the ramp.

I always take the ramp.

Centered in the middle of the lobby, it's a slow, winding climb around the chapel to my second-floor office. And the chapel is, of course, the first place I want to visit. Yes, my secretary's waiting. Yes, there are piles on my desk demanding attention. Yes, I have an interview at 10:30 a.m. But I can't clear my head of those jags in my back until I spend a moment with God. It's a moment that always includes a word of thanks that I'm here ... and a prayer for healing from the pain.

I proceed to the second floor, where on each of the three landings, a Bible verse has been inscribed in large flowing script on walls of soft lavender.

Three turns in the ramp. Three landings. Three verses.

The first one reminds me of my purpose—why I get out of bed, go through an elaborate morning routine to get ready for the day, and endure fresh visitations of pain on my commute to the center. It's why we're all here at Joni and Friends—to go out, find the disabled, and bring them in.

> But when you give a banquet, invite the poor,
> the crippled, the lame, the blind, and you will be
> blessed. (Luke 14:13–14)

Around the next turn in the ramp, at the second landing, the second wall speaks to me of God's provision for the task He has placed before me—and reminds me that His special favor rests on those who are weak.

> "My gracious favor is all you need. My power
> works best in your weakness!" So now I am glad
> to boast about my weaknesses, so that the power
> of Christ may work through me. (2 Cor. 12:9 NLT)

And the last verse at the last turn assures me that my Lord will soon come again, gathering His scattered family and mending what has been long broken.

> And when He comes, He will open the eyes of
> the blind and unstop the ears of the deaf. The
> lame will leap like a deer, and those who cannot
> speak will shout and sing! (Isa. 35:5–6 NLT)

That's the verse, right there on the third landing, that always brings tears. Because my time in the chapel didn't dissipate the spear thrusts in my hip and lower back. It's still there as I write these words—and yes, it's getting worse. Today may be yet another day when I work from the little bed in my office rather than from my wheelchair.

Did God hear my cry for help and healing in the chapel today? I'm sure He did. But for reasons He knows best, the throbbing persists.

How long will this pattern continue? How many more days of pain piercing me at every stoplight on my commute, following me around three slow turns up the ramp to my office? Of course I can't know that. But those verses on three successive walls, at three successive landings, painted there long before this current season of elevated physical stress, continue to speak to me, continue to illuminate the path ahead, and continue to help me keep on keeping on, for yet one more day.

First landing: "Give a banquet … invite the poor … you will be blessed."

In other words, *My daughter, keep on going in My name to the broken, discouraged, and despairing. Keep on being My hands and feet and eyes and ears for those who are without. Do this as long as you are able.*

Second turn: "My gracious favor is all you need. My power works best in your weakness!"

My daughter, I have not forgotten your need. I have not overlooked your hurt, disregarded your pain, closed My ears to your cry for help, or in any way withheld My favor from you. I will provide for you, and I will continue to show My might through your weakest moments, honoring your faintest attempts to honor and serve Me.

And the final turn: "And when He comes … the lame will leap like a deer!"

I come. Watch for Me! The help for which you pray—more help than you can conceive—is just around the corner. Just over the horizon. Can you see? The clouds are already beginning to part. I am coming with gifts of health and

strength and joy and life like an artesian fountain. I am making all things
new.

Three turns in the ramp, three landings, three reminders from the Word that is forever fresh and new. What's life all about for me in these days of sometimes blinding pain?

Mission, provision, and hope. A task that still needs doing, a promise that still holds true, and a hope that keeps me glancing toward the horizon.

For now, for today, it is enough.

SIX

HOW CAN I BRING HIM GLORY?

*Love means doing all we can, at whatever
cost to ourselves, to help people be enthralled
with the glory of God. When they are, they
are satisfied and God is glorified. Therefore
loving people and glorifying God are one.*
—John Piper

If God chooses to heal me of this two-year wrestling match with con-
tinual pain, I will give Him great glory. (Oh boy, you just watch!)

But if for His own good, unfathomable reasons, He chooses to allow
the anguish—this sharp, deep, thorn in my flesh—to remain in some form
until He finally issues my boarding pass for heaven (I want a window seat),
then I will also pour my life into bringing glory to His most precious,
saving, healing, holy name.

I *will!*

But how do I do that? How do any of us do that when we find ourselves in prolonged, unwelcome seasons of sorrow, stress, illness, financial
loss, relational grief—or any of life's sundry valleys and heartaches?

And what does it even mean to "give God glory," anyway?

In the Old Testament the principle word for glory seems to indicate "weight" or "heaviness." Its primary uses convey the idea of some external, physical manifestation of dignity, preeminence, or majesty. The principle New Testament word makes reference to "brightness, brilliance, and splendor."[1] There are plenty of textbook definitions out there, and I could give you one of those, but you could look it up just as easily yourself.

Just for a moment, allow me to combine the Old and New Testament concepts of glory to make a simple observation. When we glorify the name of our God, He gives us the opportunity of adding weight or significance—including adulation, respect, and honor—to His reputation. He allows us the unspeakable privilege of showcasing the brightness and splendor of His great name in our dark world.

Oh, so much more could be said about *that* of course—thousands of volumes with eye-straining print wouldn't do the subject justice. But just for now, let's allow my simple definition to suffice.

I believe that my ministries over the past forty years—through writing, speaking, painting, singing, counseling, and being an advocate for disabled people—have brought weight to the mighty name of Jesus. And I am so very glad for that.

But let's play a little "what if" game here. What if ... because of encroaching pain or even more profound disability, I became hindered from doing any or all of those well-loved activities. What then? Could I still bring Him glory? Could I still somehow, in some way, add weight to His most worthy name? Could I still prompt my Savior and friend to smile and nod with recognition over something I might try for His sake and for the love of Him?

Yes, I firmly believe that to be so.

And since I believe there is really nothing more important in all of our lives that we could do, let me suggest just a few ideas on the subject as we move past the midpoint of this book.

How Do We Bring Christ Glory in a Time of Trial or Limitation?

1. Breathe in His presence.

A few years ago I struggled through a long bout against double pneumonia. It would have been a difficult time for anyone, but for someone with quadriplegia.... Well, it was nothing short of a nightmare.

I was hospitalized for nine days, and frankly, there were times when I wondered if this might be the time God would take me home. Try to imagine lying flat and not being able to raise your head and cough when you feel that tightness and gurgling in your bronchioles. Imagine not being able to sit up in bed or at least rise up on your elbows. Sometimes it felt as if there was an invisible hand pressing an invisible pillow over my face.

On some of the worse nights, my wonderful husband put two chairs together in my hospital room and slept by my bed so I could at least quiet my heart knowing someone was there to help sit me up every time I needed to expel phlegm.

One day during my hospital stay my doctor did a very helpful thing. He set up an oxygen tank by my bed so I could breathe a little easier in those moments when I felt like I was being asphyxiated. Never did I appreciate oxygen so much! On nights when I could hardly get a breath, they slipped that oxygen mask over my face and … what relief!

Up until that illness I inhaled and exhaled with hardly a thought. Breathe in, breathe out. Who even thinks about it? But in the hospital I discovered that, whether we realize it or not, we truly live our lives moment by moment, breath by breath.

We breathe in so naturally; it's a given. But I have learned that it's more than a given. It's a gift! Oxygen is the life and breath of our body.

I have to admit, this take-something-precious-for-granted sort-of thing is often the way I relate to Jesus, our true life and breath. Because we live, move, and have our being in Him, as it says in Acts 17:28, it's all too easy to take His life-sustaining grace for granted. Every day we breathe in His love, breathe in His grace, breathe in His help.

And what do we exhale? A dull forgetfulness of His constant love toward us. The presence of God almost seems monotonous in a way; we become dead to the reality that apart from Him, we can't do a thing (John 15:5).

People who get into this bored, distracted, shallow frame of mind cease to give God the glory He deserves. The book of Malachi contains the sad, poignant story of a time in Israel's history when the Lord's own priests—the very ones charged with protecting and promoting His glory—had so fallen out of love with God that they ceased to honor Him at all. Bored and cynical, they offered sick and diseased animals on His altar—the dregs of their livestock that had no worth or value to anyone. And after offering such things, they would say, "This is contemptible," or "What a burden this is." You can picture them yawning or looking at their watches as they took their turns in God's holy temple. If it had been today, they would have been texting their friends or playing games on their iPhones.

God had to actually remind them that He is "a great king" and that His name is "feared among the nations" (1:14). But these supposed representatives of the Holy One of Israel had become so indifferent and casual about their relationship with Him that He had to seek His glory elsewhere.

We can't afford to be complacent about God's glory. The fact is that putting your Christian life on autopilot is the same thing as "walking in the flesh." When we become unaware, when we take something so precious for granted, our prayers become tedious, witnessing becomes dry, jobs become lackluster, and relationships sag under the weight of selfishness. What's worse, our communion with our Savior and best friend turns into a chore. The Lord Himself seems to lose vitality in our estimation; He becomes little more than a wooden icon in our hearts, a mere measuring rod for our behavior—someone who purchased our salvation once upon a time, someone in whom we believe in a general, distracted sort of way.

In short, we no longer give Him glory.

How does that happen? It happens when we neglect to inhale His life and breath through our waking hours. It happens when we take our Savior for granted. Oh, how could we take so great a salvation for granted?

Nothing is more mechanical than when we attempt to live a supernatural life apart from God. This is why the apostle tells us in Romans 6:11 to "count yourselves ... alive to God in Christ Jesus." To "count" means to take a daily inventory, to consciously consider yourself *alive*. I'm alive—we're alive—to God in Christ Jesus.

Jesus is the breath of life we reach for every moment of every day. Inhale His love—*no matter what your current situation or circumstances*—and you can't help but exhale gratitude and gratefulness. This is something I can do even when I am bound to my bed or trying to navigate my way through the narrow corridors of oppressive pain.

I may not be able to do a lot of things when I am suffering intense pain, but I *can* still breathe in His presence and exhale my thanks. I can still breathe in His grace and forgiveness and exhale my gratitude and love. I can still inhale His kindness and moment-by-moment help; I can still exhale acknowledgment that He is with me.

As I do, though sometimes no one but the angels may see, I am adding weight to His reputation and brightness to His splendor. And that makes my life infinitely worthwhile.

2. Don't despise the discipline of the Lord.

It's something I've brooded over a lot: *Could this pain I'm going through be God's way of disciplining me?* It's a tough question, and yes, I'm convinced that much of the suffering we go through is God's way of disciplining us. Notice I didn't say "punish." The punishment for all my wrongdoing was taken care of by Jesus on His cross. He endured the wrath of God for my sins so that I wouldn't have to.

Nevertheless, God loves me too much to let me wallow in my wrongdoing without some sort of consequence. That means I'll occasionally feel the rod—ouch!—of God's discipline. We might not like the idea, and we might even despise it. It hurts when we feel the hand of God's reproof and correction. But Hebrews 12:7–9 has some wise counsel:

> Endure hardship as discipline; God is treating you as sons. For what son is not disciplined by his father? If you are not disciplined (and everyone undergoes discipline), then you are illegitimate children and not true sons. Moreover, we have all had human fathers who disciplined us and we respected them for it. How much more should we submit to the Father of our spirits and live!

I often think of that passage of Scripture when I'm at my art easel. The paintings I love the most are always the ones I put through the toughest discipline. I bruise and batter the preliminary drawings with lots of erasures and corrections. I push my brushes to perform impossible strokes on the canvas. I demand a great deal from the oil paints I mix together, expecting colors that are so subtle you can't even find them on the color wheel. Every painting I love, I put through the wringer. But these are the paintings people most admire once they're framed and displayed on the wall in the lobby of Joni and Friends.

Not all suffering is God's discipline, and if you're like me, you tend to cringe at the idea of God correcting or reproving you. But I've got some great advice; or, I should say, God has. It's "that word of encouragement that addresses you as sons: 'My son, do not make light of the Lord's discipline, and do not lose heart when he rebukes you, because the Lord disciplines those he loves'" (Heb. 12:5–6).

First, don't do the extreme of *making light of* your hardship, thinking that it's just a small matter that you can handle by yourself and that you don't need any help, especially God's. Don't be a stoic. Or a martyr. It will only make matters worse. Rather, ask God to show you how you can work together with His Spirit to fulfill His purpose in your life.

On the other extreme, *don't lose heart*—don't emotionally crumble or cave in, thinking that God's out to get you or that He has a short fuse and will stay angry forever. God is *not* out to get you. He's not a killjoy, holding out on your healing until you shape up and start living right. He's not a big ogre, twisting your arm with more suffering until you cry "uncle!" Ask God to remove any tinge of unhealthy fear you may harbor toward Him and His discipline.

So back to my original question: Is my pain God's way of disciplining me? All I can say is the love of God is *only* after what is pure and praiseworthy in my life. And when it comes to His discipline, He *only* has my best interest at heart: that the image of Jesus would beautifully and radiantly shine in my character—in yours, too. So if the pain and discomfort of your difficult circumstances persist, don't take it lightly. But more importantly, don't lose heart. God's up to something pretty special in your life!

3. Stay supercharged.

Not long ago my fellow passengers and I were forced to change planes. Since there was no accessible bus transport to take us to the other side of the terminal, I had to wheel all the way around to the other side of the airport. By the time I got to the gate, my wheelchair batteries were nearly dead. (And it didn't help that I had forgotten to charge them the night before.)

Believe me, that taught me a lesson: Always keep those batteries powered up!

It's a lesson that goes much deeper than power wheelchairs. Just as my DieHard batteries have to have full power to take me through the day, I have to live the same way as a Christian. I simply can't approach the day with a ho-hum attitude thinking I need only so much of God's power to make it through. The Lord wants me—wants you—to remain fully charged.

"Don't burn out; keep yourselves fueled and aflame. Be alert servants of the Master, cheerfully expectant. Don't quit in hard times; pray all the harder" (Rom. 12:11–12 MSG).

Another translation reads: "Let us not allow slackness to spoil our work and let us keep the fires of the spirit burning, as we do our work for the LORD."[2]

In other words, don't let your fuel burn down. Don't let your light be shaded or covered over. Don't allow your batteries to be drained.

We see an example of this attitude in Acts 6. The church needed some deacons who would serve tables and distribute food. So they chose seven men, and Stephen was one of them. Now Stephen, in that chapter, is described as a man "full of faith and the Holy Spirit." A couple verses further on, he is described as a man "full of God's grace and power."

In other words, Stephen's spiritual fuel tank was on "full." The batteries of his soul were charged to the max. But why? You wouldn't think a young man who only served tables and distributed food would really need to be supercharged with God's power. The last time I checked, waiting on tables and handing out food parcels to the widows isn't rocket science. These are everyday, ordinary sorts of tasks, right?

But Stephen—bless his heart and thank God for his example—didn't dare go into the day without keeping in step with the Spirit, without feeding on the Word and filling up in prayer. The result? This man was no average deacon. Because God's power overflowed in his life, his behind-the-scenes service resulted in the chance to revolution-ize the church. His witness was so irresistibly powerful that the Jewish leaders could find no way to oppose him. They had to talk others into lying about him, which led to his arrest—which led to one of the bold-est, most powerful messages in the entire Bible.

Don't allow the enemy of your soul to convince you that your tasks today are ho-hum and ordinary, nothing special, nothing extraordinary. Keep your batteries charged and you can't help but have a powerful influence on others. Fully charged, like Stephen, you will be anything but average.

And you will bring God glory.

4. Keep a humble heart.

Don't you love the way God finds ways to keep us humble and depen-dent upon Him?

I can't say that I always appreciate the process, but I do value the results! You know what I'm talking about here: You're going along fine, looking good, coming across okay, got your act together, and then—bam!—circumstances knock the props out from under you, and you fall flat on your face. It happened to me (yet again) not long ago.

I was getting ready for a speaking engagement at a prestigious conference. It was one of those exclusive kinds of things, and I knew there would be a lot of corporate executives there—trustees from various foundations and colleges, and presidents of universities. I had worked extra hard on my message, trying to get things "just right." I not only went out and bought myself a new outfit to wear, but I asked my girlfriend to clean and polish my wheelchair. I wanted this presentation to be perfect.

Three days before I was to leave for the conference, however, something occurred that has never happened before. I was wheeling outside and began to feel a thump-thump-thump-thump. I looked down over my shoulder, and much to my horror, the tire of my wheelchair had split apart. All the foam that was inside was beginning to bulge and spill out like a big, ugly growth on the side of my tire. It looked awful—and I knew if I didn't do something fast, I'd soon be riding on the rims of my wheels.

When I showed the problem to Ken, he immediately went after his beloved roll of silver duct tape. I looked at him in disbelief. "Duct tape? You're going to fix my tire with *duct tape?*" He explained that until we could get a new tire, it was our only option. So he proceeded to tightly wrap my tire in layer after layer of duct tape (seemingly enjoying himself)—round and round my wheel it went until the bulge was contained.

"Okay," Ken said. "Try wheeling on it."

I slowly powered my wheelchair forward. It was still going thump-thump-thump-thump, but at least this time the rim was safe. *But it looked absolutely tacky.* When my girlfriend saw it, she said, "Hmmm. Well, Joni, think of it as, um … tire jewelry."

I have to confess that my first thought was, *Oh, no. I can't believe I've got to go to the conference looking like this—like I've got a gross tumor on my tire!*

But no sooner did that unworthy thought cross my mind than I realized that this was simply God's way of keeping me humble. Maybe for other people He allows a coffee stain on their shirt, spinach between their front teeth, or dandruff all over their black sweater. For me, it was a lumpy, uncool, immediately visible duct-tape bandage on my wheelchair tire.

It's amazing how a silly thing like that can reveal how self-focused you have been. But the Lord was gracious to me in spite of my vanity. Ken was able to make a couple of quick calls, and I got a new tire before heading off to the conference. Was I relieved! But once there, I was ever mindful of Deuteronomy 8:16: "He … [humbled and tested] you so that in the end it might go well with you."

The simple fact is that I can't be about glorifying myself—adding weight and luster to my own name and reputation—and the Lord at the same time. In Isaiah 42:8 He tells us, "I am the LORD; that is my name! I will not give my glory to another."

So if He allows humbling circumstances in my life, I know He does so for good reason. With Peter, I will humble myself under God's mighty hand, that He may lift me up in due time.[3]

5. Maintain a childlike wonder about life.

I recently spent the afternoon with a friend who has an eighteen-month-old little boy. Benjamin is a blue-eyed, towheaded, precocious, all-boy kind of child. He loves balls and blocks. But most of all, he loves life.

He knows several words, but the phrase that most often tumbles out is, "Oh, wow!"

Show him a new squeaky toy, and it's, "Oh, wow!" Or take him for a short stroll down the sidewalk only to discover a caterpillar and, again, it's another, "Oh, wow!" Everything is, "Oh, wow!" For Benjamin, all of life is new, exciting, and awe-inspiring—like a birthday present just out of its wrappings. Wonders wait around every corner. Objects and animals, grass and sky, other children, and even visitors in wheelchairs amaze and delight him. He seems to gulp down life with extreme gusto!

As I watched Ben's unfettered enthusiasm over seeing ducks, balls, and bugs on the sidewalk, I thought how great it would be if we could maintain the same, "Oh, wow!" attitude about who God is and what He's done.

David, perhaps still a young man out in the Judean wilderness with his father's sheep, gazed up into the Milky Way at night and wrote these words:

> When I look up into the night skies and see the work of your fingers—the moon and the stars you have made—I cannot understand how you can bother with mere puny man, to pay any attention to him! (Ps. 8:3–4 TLB)

And again:

> The heavens declare the glory of God;
>   the skies proclaim the work of his hands.
> Day after day they pour forth speech;
>   night after night they display knowledge.
> There is no speech or language
>   where their voice is not heard. (Ps. 19:1–3)

I'm not sure what the ancient Hebrew equivalent of, "Oh, wow!" might be, but I have to believe David breathed those words, lost in the wonder of his God's majestic handiwork.

Surely the apostle Paul had such a moment when he wrote in his letter to the Romans: "What a wretched man I am! Who will rescue me from this body of death?" Then he answers his own question by saying, "Thanks be to God…. There is now no condemnation for those who are in Christ Jesus."[4]

In other words, "Oh, wow!"

A little bit later in Romans, he writes: "For I am convinced that neither death nor life, neither angels nor demons, neither the present nor the future, nor any powers, neither height nor depth, nor anything else in all creation, will be able to separate us from the love of God that is in Christ Jesus our Lord."[5]

That's another one that has me gaping like Benjamin, thinking, *This is too much to wrap my mind around! Wow, this is great!*

Cultivating that kind of huge appreciation for life—the kind that seems to come so naturally to little Benjamin—and possessing that sense of wonder is really a gift. You can't work it up, drum it up, and you certainly can't fake it. To enjoy—really enjoy—the works of God and His character to the point where "Oh, wow!" comes only one way: The less we make of ourselves, the greater God seems. And the more we make of God, the more we get into His Word and think whatsoever thoughts are pure, honest, and praiseworthy, the more we'll find ourselves saying, "Oh, wow!"

Cynicism will neutralize that sense of wonder in a trice; a crabby, ungrateful spirit will deny it admittance to our heart. But if we truly set ourselves to glorify our God like David, or like little Benjamin, the sheer joy of living will grow again like a shy, fragile wildflower—even in the most hostile of terrains.

6. Serve wholeheartedly.

This morning when I greeted my girlfriend who came to get me dressed and in my wheelchair, the first thing I said to her was, "Oh, boy! We get to serve Jesus today!"

Dana laughed.

But, hey, it's the way I *have* to wake up, pain or no pain. I *can't* be glum or sour or peevish, even if I am a little tired of paralysis, and even if I am weary of chronic pain. God's got me alive—I'm still here!—and that means there's a purpose for my life, a race to run, and a plan for my life. God has ordained this day for me to bring Him glory as best I can and to serve Him with joy.

So today, in spite of everything, to the best of my ability leaning on Him, it's, "Oh, boy! I get to serve the Lord today!"

Did you know that kind of attitude is a command? Psalm 100 says, "Serve the Lord with gladness." In other words, it's not an option. Serving Him with gladness isn't a nice suggestion, as if God were saying, "Oh, by the way, when you serve Me today, would you please smile just a little? It would really mean a lot to Me. It would be just great if you could get your attitude in line." No, serving the Lord with gladness is not something He would *like* us to do (if we happen to think about it or feel in the mood); it's something we're commanded to do.

Whoever you are, whatever your circumstances today, God commands joyfulness in your kingdom service. And that directive applies whether you're a quadriplegic in a wheelchair, a parent picking up or dropping off kids at school, a student going to class, a resident in a nursing home, or someone getting ready to lead a Bible study. It counts for people in full-time ministry, homemakers, dishwashers, and meter maids. As a son or daughter of God, whatever He has you doing *is* service in His name. And He says whatever you do, do it heartily (I like that word, *heartily,* because it means *happily*) unto Him. Serve the Lord with gladness, with happiness. It's not an option.

Listen to what God says to His people in Deuteronomy 28:47–48: "Because you did not serve the Lord your God joyfully and gladly … you will serve the enemies the Lord sends against you."

My friends, it's not enough that you serve the Lord. You must serve Him joyfully and gladly. He is completely displeased with anything less. I would go so far as to say, given Deuteronomy 28, that He won't even bless such service when performed with a sour, bored, irritated, or resentful disposition.

As I write these words, I can't help but think of my new friend, Pam, who lives in a home for girls who are seeking to leave the streets.

The home, in downtown Hollywood, provides a safe place and a refuge for young women who have fled prostitution and drug dealing on some of the meaner streets in "Tinseltown." Elsie, who runs the home, walks those streets, shares the gospel, and leads these girls to Christ. If these new converts truly desire to change their lives and commit to new responsibilities, they have a place in Elsie's home.

Pam is one such new believer. Although a Christian with a sweet spirit, she bears the scars of knife fights and heroin needles. Her arms are marred and marked with tattoos. But this is one unusual believer. I was immediately struck by her genuine and overflowing joy when she explained to me her new role in Elsie's home.

"I scrub the toilets and the bathrooms!" she exclaimed with great enthusiasm. "That's my job, and I love it!" Pam was so grateful to have structure in her life, safety in her surroundings, and an honest-to-goodness job serving in Christ's kingdom.

When I watched her go about her duties that day I visited Elsie's home, I thought of Psalm 84:10, where it says, "Better is one day in your courts than a thousand elsewhere; I would rather be a doorkeeper in the house of my God than dwell in the tents of the wicked." I guess Pam could paraphrase, *"A day in Elsie's home is better than a thousand on the street, and I would rather clean toilets under the roof of this godly woman than dwell in the flophouses on the boulevard."*

I was deeply impressed by Pam's humble, happy spirit toward her job. Her delight in cleaning toilets sprang from a keen awareness of her role in the body of Christ. Few of you reading these words have a background like Pam's, but every day, each of us rolls up our sleeves to accomplish menial tasks. It could be changing oil at Jiffy Lube, changing ink cartridges in printers, changing the sheets in motel rooms, or even changing a diaper on a little one or on an elderly parent. Like Pam, when you and I consider these jobs as service to Christ, we discover the joy of being "a doorkeeper in the house of God." It's just a way of living out Paul's words in 1 Corinthians 10: "Whether we eat or drink, whatever we do … do it all for the glory of God."

A day of ministry in Christ's kingdom is far better than a thousand days lived in pursuit of self-destructive pleasures.

And for me (please hear me, my friend, and weigh the import of these words), *a day in this wheelchair serving Him, a day representing Him though in the grip of this unrelenting pain, is better than a thousand self-fulfilled days lived pain free and on my feet.* It's a lesson people like Pam and me are learning every day.

7. Pour out your all.

One of my favorite stories in Scripture is the one about Mary of Bethany and how she poured out her vial of priceless perfume on the Lord Jesus.

I have wondered about that perfume….

I wonder how long it had been sitting on the shelf in the home of Mary, Martha, and Lazarus. Was it tucked away in a little wooden chest for safekeeping, like something to bank on for a rainy day? Was it on a shelf covered with a fine film of dust, a shelf so high up that it could only be reached with a stool or ladder? Was it a family heirloom, treasured and protected, handed down from parents or grandparents?

Maybe that vial of expensive perfume was being saved for the next generation.

There seems to be no doubt that it was Mary's alone to give. We read of no objection from Martha or Lazarus when she poured it out on their dearest Friend. It was up to Mary what to do with it.

She could have kept it to herself, of course. It could have remained on the shelf, collecting dust rather than being broken open and poured on the Lord Jesus. But then the Savior would have gone to the cross with no lingering fragrance of a godly woman's sacrificial love, and Mary's story would have never been told to numberless multitudes in countless languages and dialects all over the world.

I'm so glad that Mary didn't save her special treasure for a rainy day. I'm so grateful she didn't decide to leave it locked in a cask like an untouchable family heirloom. I'm so thankful she broke it open and poured it out on the one and only one who was worth it all and more.

What Mary did with that perfume speaks to me. There is something about "pouring it all out" in service, dedication, and love to Christ that makes your life truly fragrant. And not only your life—*you* become a fragrant offering, reminding the Father of all that Jesus sacrificed when *He* walked on earth. There's something sweet and precious about cracking open your heart and giving your affection to the Savior in the midst of a difficult or painful situation that takes a simple testimony like yours and pushes it over the top. *Because there's nothing like a song of praise rising out of brokenness that brings glory to our God.*

In the process, it also opens a wellspring of joy and gladness about life.

Friend, what are you holding onto tightly? What gift or resource or talent have you squirreled away for safekeeping? What are you saving or holding back from being poured out as a sacrificial offering of praise and thanksgiving to the Lord? Yes, I do believe all of us have special, heaven-sent talents we can use to promote God's name and reputation. In addition, you've got some gratitude you can show, thanksgiving you can pour out, smiles you can give, time and treasure you can offer, and words of encouragement you can share with a needy soul.

Don't bottle them up.

Don't leave your love sealed, "safe" and placed on a high shelf.

Don't save your smiles and your friendship for those you know or like or "feel comfortable with."

Give gratitude in the midst of hardship, and you'll find it will be like pouring out perfume on the Lord Himself. It'll be a sacrifice of praise and thanksgiving, sweet and fragrant, that will bring great glory to the Savior.

Just recently, as I was reading in Matthew 25, the following little paraphrase took shape in my mind.

> Then the King will say to those on his right, "Come, you who are blessed by my Father; take your inheritance, the kingdom prepared for you since the creation of the world. For I was discouraged, and you gave Me a smile of encouragement and a kind word.... I was grieving and you sent Me a note and bouquet of spring flowers.... I was confused and anxious, and you took me to Starbucks and gave me your counsel over a caramel macchiato.... I was lonely, and you took Me out to lunch at IHOP.... I was frightened about preparing my taxes, but you showed Me what to do and where to go.... I was a child who wanted to get out of the city and go to Bible camp, and you paid My way."

Then the righteous will answer him, "Lord, when did we see You discouraged and speak kindly to You? When did we send You flowers or take You to Starbucks or buy You lunch? When did we help you with Your taxes or pay Your way to Bible camp?"

The King will reply, "I tell you the truth, whatever you did for one of the least of these brothers and sisters of mine, you did for Me."

8. Don't hold back on life.

The other day my friend Karen flew into town from the East Coast to see me.

No big deal, right?

Well, really it is a big deal. Because Karen came by herself, and she is almost completely blind. With a lot of courage and plain old determination, she got on the plane, found a friend to pick her up at the airport, looked me up, and came to see me.

On the night of her arrival, the two of us went out to dinner at a local restaurant. I had thought she was going to ask her friend to join us, but the friend had to get going and explained she was only there to drop Karen off.

It gave me a little pause. There would be no one to give us assistance at the restaurant? A blind woman and a paralyzed woman? This was going to be somewhat interesting. When Karen's friend took off and left us, I think the staff at the restaurant was as nervous about it as I was.

Karen, however, was all smiles. It was going to be no problem at all.

Once we got settled, I had to give instructions to my friend. "Reach into the back of my pack, get my special spoon, and please tuck it in the little cuff right here on my arm splint. Thanks. Good. And could you put the napkin in my lap, push my glass of water near you where you can hold it to my mouth for me—you're not going to knock it over, are you?"

I don't mind telling you that some of the other diners seemed a little edgy watching us get ready for our meal. I saw someone eyeing us when Karen—bless her heart—found the water glass, put both hands around it, and lifted the straw—with my verbal directions—to my mouth.

In spite of ourselves, we had to laugh.

"Is this the blind leading the paralyzed?" she asked.

"No," I said, still laughing. "This is the paralyzed leading the blind, because I have to tell you where your food is on the plate!"

After awhile, people stopped staring. I think it was because they saw how relaxed we were, despite the circus. I also think they were just a little bit blessed to see a blind woman and a wheelchair-bound quadriplegic enjoying one another's company. And maybe they wondered just a bit more when they saw us bow our heads and pray out loud to the Father together.

It was a witness, and I believe it brought our Lord glory.

He is our strength, He is our courage, He is our enabler, He is the source of our joy. And yes, we got through the meal without spilling any food on the floor or water on the table. (Although I did have to ask the waiter to take my spoon out my arm splint, wipe it off, and put it in my backpack.)

Life, my friend, is an adventure. Karen said that night, "Joni, my disability is worsening, and I know that one day I may not be able to do this stuff—fly by myself and have a dinner alone with a friend. So I'm going to make the most of the time I've got and do what I can with what little I've got left."

In the course of some of these recent days as I've fought for just the smallest bits of normalcy and peace in my war with pain, I don't feel as if I have very much left to offer at all.

But in the final scheme of things, I know it doesn't matter.

He is the one who will make the most of the little I've got. He is the one who took note of the widow's mite, dropped into the treasury, and affirmed that her little was worth more in heaven's sight than the offering of those who had given much, but had much more held in reserve.

SEVEN

HOW DO I REGAIN MY PERSPECTIVE?

People who look through keyholes are apt to get
the idea that most things are keyhole shaped.
—Author Unknown

I picture an early morning just before sunrise—the cooing of doves, the call of a distant quail, the murmur of rushing water, and the soft crunch of two pairs of sandaled feet in fine gravel.

The prophet and his son walk slowly up to the end of the aqueduct, where the water spills into the Upper Pool; at that very moment, the king of Judah steps down from his chariot.

I imagine the king looking up in surprise, not expecting to see anyone out there on the road to the Washerman's Field—let alone *Isaiah*, the legendary prophet of Jehovah, counselor to his father and grandfather.

Has the king slipped away from his royal entourage to think through a national crisis, or is he simply checking the water supply and wondering how to protect it from enemy hands? The Bible doesn't say.

But we do know that this meeting is no accident.

God has specifically told Isaiah to meet the king in this very place, at this very time, and with a specific message.

For a moment (I'm still imagining), no one says a word. The king watches as a morning breeze stirs the old prophet's long, silvery hair and beard. Ahaz has a right to be wary! So many times, God's prophets brought fiery messages of impending judgment. But on this day Isaiah bears a word the young king very much needs to hear. This word of the Lord *should* bring comfort and reassurance to his heart, but will he have enough faith to receive it? Will he allow the word of God to actually change his view of reality?

It's a question for every one of us.

Will we allow the truth of God's promises to change the way we see life, with all its challenges and obstacles? To ease our fears and calm our anxieties? To give us hope and confidence when there doesn't seem to be any earthly reason for either?

One thing the Bible seems to do over and over again is take a man or woman's view and perspective of a given situation and lay it alongside God's view of the same situation. And the contrast? Well, sometimes it makes you wonder if the people and God could really be looking at the same circumstance!

Newly crowned King Ahaz, a young man barely out of his teens, inherited the throne of Judah at a time very much like today, in our own nation. Frightening news reports and scary headlines had everyone in Judah on edge. The word was that Aram, or Syria, had just allied itself with Judah's other major enemy at that time, the northern kingdom of Israel. Together they had plans to attack Jerusalem, kill the king, and carve up the tiny kingdom for themselves.

When news of the alliance hit Jerusalem, you might have expected a massive prayer meeting. But no. Instead, there was panic in the streets—and panic in the palace. The Bible says "the hearts of Ahaz and his people were shaken, as the trees of the forest are shaken by the wind" (Isa. 7:2).

Two enemies joining together against little Judah? How could they defend themselves against such odds? How could they survive? What would happen? They felt utterly overwhelmed.

Have you been there? Or maybe I should put it like this: Have you been there *lately?* Have you looked at the situations in your life and felt weak in the knees by what you see? What you thought had been a secure retirement has been seriously eroded by the stock-market slide. *How will you care for yourself in your old age?* Your children have turned away from the good paths you taught them as little ones and seem determined to walk in a destructive direction. *What will happen to them?* The lab report comes to you in the mail, sandwiched between your phone bill and a pizza coupon. They've found the presence of cancer in one of the tests, and you're to make a follow-up appointment. *Will this be a death sentence?*

Sometimes the challenges and burdens of life look impossibly huge. You feel as if you're looking up at some towering mountain directly in the path where you have to walk.

That's how King Ahaz felt that morning at the aqueduct. How do we know that? Because through His prophet, God immediately set out to calm the young man's heart:

> Be careful, keep calm, and don't be afraid. Do not
> lose heart. (Isa. 7:4)

Say *what?* Not be afraid? Are you kidding? With two enemy armies on the march? With rumors and threats darkening the horizon like an approaching storm?

That was the moment God chose to issue the king an amazing invitation. And I believe it is an invitation He extends to every one of us at different times in our lives. Isaiah invited Ahaz to change his perspective for a moment and look at the same situation *through God's eyes* rather than his own. And boy did the picture look different! The Lord said, "Do not lose heart because of these two smoldering stubs of firewood...." And of the expected invasion, God said, "It will not take place, it will not happen" (vv. 4, 7).

Ahaz was seeing these two kings aligned against him as a giant forest fire, consuming everything in its path. But from God's point of view, they were only two smoldering stubs of firewood ... black and charred, used up, all but burned out.

Then the Lord had one more word for the timid king: *"If you do not stand firm in your faith, you will not stand at all."*[1]

God won't always change our circumstances, but if we ask Him, He will often step in to change our perspective! He will help us catch a glimpse of life through the eyes of faith, as He sees it. And that glimpse is worth everything.

In the following few pages, I'd like to suggest several ways that may help us gain that fresh perspective we so desperately need. And just in case you really feel lost in the dark, let me begin with three very simple steps that will send you on your way.

A Place to Start

I have to admit that the timid King Ahaz and I have had a lot in common through the years.

Sometimes I look into the future and just feel ... overwhelmed. Try as I might, I can't seem to see beyond my fears. The path ahead of me seems fogged in by anxiety.

You know how it goes. Sometimes all it takes is a phone call, email, or piece of bad news to send you off the path of faith into the shadows of worry and doubt.

That's what happened to me not long ago when I got word that a coworker's best friend—she can't be more than sixty-one or sixty-two—had been diagnosed with Alzheimer's. I thought, *At her age?* It jarred me. I began to think, *Boy, that's not far from my age. What does God have in store for me?*

There's hardly a Christian who hasn't looked into the future and thought, *What's God's will for me? What will He do? How will things work out? What's His plan for the rest of my life?* You don't have to be in your sixties to be asking that question. Most people ask it in their twenties or even younger than that.

For whatever your age or life situation, I'd like to suggest 1 Thessalonians 5:16–18—short and sweet as it may be—as a place to start when you need a perspective change.

> Be joyful always; pray continually; give thanks in
> all circumstances, for this is God's will for you in
> Christ Jesus.

It sounds a little like the Lord's counsel to young King Ahaz, doesn't it? *Be careful. Keep calm. Don't be afraid. Don't lose heart.* Do you find yourself struggling to discern God's will when your problems begin to close in on you? Paul's succinct counsel will serve you very well—no matter what your situation might be.

- Be joyful always.
- Pray continually.
- Give thanks in all circumstances.

That's certainly enough to get a person started in finding the will of God. In fact, you could work on those three things the rest of your life and still never master them.

"Ah, but Joni," you say, "you don't know my situation. You have no idea! I got this call last night from my daughter.... I received this hospital bill in today's mail.... My husband's been drinking again.... There's all sorts of pain and turmoil in our family right now. How can I be thankful when I'm facing such heartaches?"

As a matter of fact, God isn't asking you to *be* thankful. He's asking you to *give* thanks. There's a big difference. One response involves emotions, the other your choices, your decisions about a situation, your intent, your "step of faith."

It takes faith—sometimes great faith in a terrible circumstance—to choose to forgive, to choose the loving (and not angry) response. That's just plain *hard*. Especially when your emotions—like a fast-running stream—are seeking to pull you in the other direction. Trusting God has nothing to do with following your feelings.

Give thanks that He is sovereign. Give thanks that He is in control. Give thanks that He's planning it all for your good—for your family's good—which ultimately will be *all* to His glory.

The threefold biblical command (because that's what it is, and nothing less) to be joyful, pray always, and give thanks will lead to a clearer understanding of where God is leading you and what He wants you to do next.

It's what happened to me many years ago after the accident that broke my neck. In that hospital in Baltimore I gritted my teeth and willfully gave thanks for everything—from the awful food to the grueling hours of physical therapy.

Months later, a miracle occurred. I began to *feel* thankful. My brighter outlook enabled me to give thanks for greater things. Then, later on, another miracle occurred. I was able to rejoice in my suffering. And finding God's will from then on out? It just seemed to naturally unfold.

Refuse to Focus on Your Fears

Ah, but those fears!

That cold sense of gnawing dread.

The anxiety that sometimes feels like a tight belt around your chest.

It's all too easy, isn't it, to get caught up in situations that make us afraid? Believe me, I know. You and I may not be facing two advancing armies as the king of Judah did, but life has plenty of other anxieties that can rob us of our peace and bring us low!

My girlfriend Jean, for instance, recently received a doctor's report that said she had scleroderma. When people around her heard the news, they said, "Sclero *what?*"

Not many people know about this troubling disease of the muscle tissue and skin. Jean certainly didn't know, and so she decided to become an expert. In the days that followed she utterly immersed herself in all the available information. She was constantly in front of her computer, researching articles, writing doctors, comparing reports, and investigating treatment options.

But as the days turned into weeks, I began to notice something about my friend. It was undoubtedly helpful that she was learning so much, but I couldn't help but notice that her focus on God began to change.

You'd ask her how she was doing with the Lord, and she'd reply with her recent medical report. She'd come to Bible study or you'd run into her at church and, well … it turned into an opportunity to bring you up to date on the latest news about scleroderma.

At first it was understandable. You'd expect Jean to be concerned about her condition. But after awhile I wondered if her faith in the Lord was beginning to suffer.

If you find yourself with a painful or limiting physical condition, there's nothing wrong with tracking down the relevant facts and treatment options. It's good to know about the diagnosis and prognosis and all the rest of it. But the lure to know more and more about your problem, and the lack of desire to know God more and more in the midst of your problem … well, that's a clear indication that your faith is becoming diminished.

Again, this is precisely where we need a divine change of perspective.

The fact is that the God who loves us doesn't allow distressing medical reports in our lives to send us down worry-choked side roads of medical minutia. No, any such crisis is meant to awaken us to the reality of God, His nearness, His care, His presence, and His ever-present help. As with all of life's disappointments and heartaches, it's meant to put force behind the directive in Hosea chapter 6, where it says, "Let us know; let us press on to know the LORD."[2]

And please remember, those words were set down at a time when the nation of Israel was being overwhelmed with problems. Hosea's prescription? Let us know ... and let us press on to know the Lord better and better.

When suffering hits us broadside, it's bound to shake our faith a little—just as if we were driving across a high bridge in a compact car and got hit by a great gust of wind. You have to make sure you have both hands on the wheel! But trials are also meant to waken us to the truth of Daniel 11:32 (ESV), where it says, "The people who know their God shall stand firm and take action."

If you're facing what seems to be an overwhelming situation in your life this week, I want to encourage you to stand firm. Don't let this thing fill up your whole horizon. Don't let your anxieties swallow you up or drain your faith dry. Rather, stand firm and take action. Take it as an opportunity to do a little research of your own into God's Word. Compare Bible verses with each other; investigate the examples of Paul or Joseph or Daniel or Peter and how they dealt with bad news and suffering in their lives.

What a waste of an illness or injury if we read—or go on talking—day and night about that illness, that injury, and not about the God who allowed it for His own sovereign reasons.

My friend Dave Powlison has some very good advice in that regard.

Dave is a professor at the Christian Counseling Education Foundation. He's also fighting a war with a cancer that seeks to ravage his body. Used to being a man on the go, Dave has been forced to slow down and learn some new lessons in patience as he walks through this unexpected season of life.

I've never had to face cancer myself, but as I've watched Dave, I have drawn so much encouragement, so much help and hope, just observing the way he approaches the challenges of this disease.

As you well know, cancer is such an alarming word; it immediately spreads fear and doubt. Dave has gone through the usual chemotherapy routines—the waiting, the uncertainty, and the awful reaction to the drugs. But I'm amazed at the way he has kept his emotional balance ... and his courage.

In the face of all the fear, pain, and sickness, just listen to what Dave wrote to me not long ago:

> Joni, I have learned that for every one sentence you say to others about your cancer, say ten sentences about your God, your hope, and what He is teaching you, and the small blessings of each day. For every hour you spend researching or discussing your cancer, spend ten hours researching and discussing and serving your Lord. Relate all that you are learning about cancer back to Him and His purposes, and you won't become obsessed [with fears and doubts].

What outstanding counsel! What powerful truth. I need to remember this special insight from Dave when I feel overwhelmed by my pain in this wheelchair. You can relate, can't you? Because when we are hit hard with suffering, our tendency is to go on and on about our problems—especially problems that relate to our health. We'll go into detail about our scleroderma, a knee surgery that's not healing, a rehabilitation program that's super hard, or even about our chemotherapy regimen.

What I need to do is learn from Dave. For every sentence I say or write about "my condition," I need to say ten sentences about the grace and strength and help and encouragement and blessings of God!

The truth is, in this world it's a 100 percent guarantee that we *will* suffer. But at the same time, Jesus Christ is 100 percent certain to meet us, encourage us, comfort us, grace us with strength and perseverance, and yes, even restore joy in our lives. Your Savior is 100 percent certain to be with you through every challenge.

The Bible tells us time and again that God is faithful, and greater is He who is in you than any ache or pain or even terminal illness.

Remember today, if you start talking about your health issues—or any problems, for that matter—be sure to talk also about the grace of our wonderful Lord to sustain and save!

A Shining Example

I just recently read something from the pen of John Piper that seemed to be written just for me.

Piper was reflecting on a situation the apostle Paul describes in Philippians chapter 2. Apparently the church in Philippi had sent out one of their number, Epaphroditus, as an emissary tasked with bringing a gift to Paul while he was in prison. According to that passage, Epaphroditus became ill and almost died while he was visiting with Paul.

So here's what Paul told the Philippians:

> But I think it is necessary to send back to you Epaphroditus, my brother, fellow worker and fellow soldier, who is also your messenger, whom you sent to take care of my needs. For he longs for all of you and is distressed because you heard he was ill. Indeed he was ill, and almost died. But God had mercy on him, and not on him only but also on me, to spare me sorrow upon sorrow.

Therefore I am all the more eager to send him, so
that when you see him again you may be glad and
I may have less anxiety. (vv. 25–28)

Finally recovering from his serious brush with death, Epaphroditus
"has been distressed *because you heard he was ill.*"

Piper writes:

What an amazing response! It does not say the
Philippians were distressed that he was ill, but
that *Epaphroditus* was distressed because they
heard he was ill. That is the kind of heart God is
aiming to create [when we suffer]: a deeply affec-
tionate, caring heart for people. Don't waste your
[suffering] by retreating into yourself.

Apparently Epaphroditus was such a caring, humble man that he didn't
want others worrying about him. He didn't want to distress his fellow
Christians, knowing that they had enough problems without being anxious
for his health. Anyway, Epaphroditus probably thought—even though he
had almost died—that his health problems were insignificant compared to
the hardships his friends had been facing.

Can't you just see him shaking his head and saying to the apostle, "Oh
man, Paul, I didn't want *this*. Tell 'em I'm better. Tell 'em I'll be fine. The
last thing they need to be worrying about these days is *my* health!"

Does that speak to you like it does to me?

Epaphroditus models a praiseworthy, wonderful perspective here, and
I hope that when I write about my disability or my battles with pain, that
I do it in such a way as to encourage others in Christ—not make them
anxious for me or worried about me. Because I'll tell you, my quadriplegia
is no big deal in comparison to what most Christians are facing in parts of

the world where there is war and persecution—and so little help for people with disabilities or heartbreaking pain.

Maybe you can identify with me a little here, but I know there are times when I talk about myself way too much. If we have a health problem, a new ache or pain, or some issue that has made walking (or in my case, wheeling) even more difficult, then we *talk* about it, don't we? Dare I use the word *grumble*?

"Lift Up Your Eyes"

I want you to join me today in asking God to help us cultivate a genuine focus on others, and less of a focus on our own pains and problems. That's a choice my friend Hannah made … and I have a strong feeling she'll never regret it.

Last night I was on the phone with Hannah, who has been struggling with three issues that sound similar to what Ahaz must have grappled with that morning by the Upper Pool.

First, she has huge doubts about the goodness of God.

Second, she has paralyzing thoughts about an unknown future.

And third, she knows that she has become terribly self-centered. She's discouraged that she can't seem to stop thinking about her own problems. It's as though she's been running the same deeply rutted track, around and around, never getting anywhere.

Hannah is old enough in the Lord to know that something's very wrong with that picture. But she also knows that she is haunted by the memories of so much abuse when she was a child—terrible sexual abuse. She said to me last night, "Joni, I feel like *I'm* the one who is really disabled, not you." I knew what she was talking about; I understood those trapped feelings—the doubts, the fears, the always-thinking-of-yourself.

I was quiet for a long moment, waiting on the Lord for words to say to her.

Suddenly I found myself picturing a little girl named Jenny.

Jenny's mother is a prostitute who lives in and out of motels and works the east end of the San Fernando Valley in California. Los Angeles social services took Jenny away from her mother when she was five years old—but by that time, the little girl had experienced serial abuse for years. They placed her with my friend Rebecca, who had already adopted Jenny's older half sister. I explained to Hannah how I had been joining in prayer for these two little girls whose personalities even now, at such young ages, are tragically damaged.

Hannah listened to all of this. Finally I asked her, "Hannah, would you please pray for Jenny? Six-year-old Jenny?"

There was a long pause—a silence on the other end of the phone. Finally Hannah said, "Of course. Yes. And let's pray for all the Jennys who don't have adoptive mothers like Rebecca."

One of us remembered the words of Jesus to His disciples: "Do you not say, 'There are yet four months, then comes the harvest'? Look, I tell you, lift up your eyes, and see that the fields are white for harvest." And, "Pray earnestly to the Lord of the harvest to send out laborers into his harvest" (John 4:35; Matt. 9:38 ESV).

There on the phone we agreed that though the need is so very great, laborers, like my friend Rebecca, are few.

It was at that very moment that Hannah experienced a divine change in perspective. Instead of seeing the overwhelming nature of her own problems, she had "lifted her eyes" beyond herself to see someone else's need.

"Joni," she said quietly, "*I* want to be one of those laborers. I want to help little girls who've gone through even worse than what I've experienced."

By the time our conversation ended last night, Hannah had taken a huge turn. She learned that the doubts, fears, and self-centeredness were really the opposite of the faith, hope, and love described in 1 Corinthians 13. She knew that she still lacked faith and hope, and still wrestled with doubts and fears. But little Jenny had shown her that the answer to self-centeredness isn't endless self-examination, but simply love—a love that reaches outside of itself, and focuses on helping those whose plight is worse than our own.

Hold onto Hope

I need all the hope I can get, and I'm not ashamed to admit it. I'm disabled, things aren't easy, and I thrive on hope. I love anything to do with hope. One contemporary paraphrase of Paul's words in Romans 15 puts it like this:

> Oh! May the God of green hope fill you up with
> joy, fill you up with peace, so that your believing
> lives, filled with the life-giving energy of the Holy
> Spirit, will brim over with hope![3]

As you and I trust God through the toughest of times, He imparts even more hope, evidenced by joy and peace of mind and heart. A Christian who is full of joy, who is peaceful about his circumstances, is the Christian who has hope. He has the God of hope front and center in his heart.

It's why I keep a certain pastel pencil drawing on my art easel—the same drawing that's been sitting on my easel for well over a year now. It's a scene of a church in the woods, covered by snow, with the mountains in the distance. I started it over a year ago, hopeful that I would be able to complete it in a short time.

But it didn't turn out that way.

Because of the pain I've been experiencing in my back, I've had to stay away from the easel for some time now; holding pencils between my teeth and leaning over at an awkward angle to draw … well, it only makes for more pain. Even so, I often find myself wheeling into my art studio to look at the unfinished sketch that's still sitting there on my easel. I refuse to put it away in my flat file.

Why? Because I'm hopeful. I believe—I really do believe—that sometime in the future, maybe in a few months, I'll be able to get back to drawing on a regular basis. My artwork is a ministry, and even if I end up only doing line sketches rather than a full-blown painting … well, that's okay.

I trust in the God of all hope. I trust that He has given me an artistic talent to use for His glory, and for the encouragement of my brothers and sisters in Christ.

I don't know when, but I know I will draw again.

That's not wishful thinking, that's hope, drawn from the deep, artesian wells of the God of hope.

Don't Look at the Wall

We began this chapter with a story about a young king who was so filled with fear that he couldn't absorb God's words of comfort and hope—even when he found himself eyeball to eyeball with the Lord's prophet.

Ahaz couldn't seem to tear his eyes away from the northern horizon, where he knew that two enemy armies would soon be massing.

My friend Dan, the race-car driver, would have some timely words for Judah's king (if he wouldn't listen to Isaiah). He would say, "Ahaz, dude, you're looking at *the wall*. Steer toward the open space!"

Dan has seen many turns around the track. I can't say I understand much about his sport—or the passion to risk life and limb traveling at the high speeds those drivers do. But I can certainly appreciate Dan's love and enthusiasm for his car and crew.

Some time ago I asked Dan about Dale Earnhardt's infamous 2001 crash, which took the NASCAR icon's life. The horrifying clip is now on YouTube, and gets plenty of hits—even after all these years. As you watch it, it's obvious Dale couldn't pull out of that plunge toward the wall. His speed and the trajectory of his car just made escape impossible. I asked Dan if that kind of thing happens often on a speedway.

"Oh yes," he said. "Guys in their cars get in a spin, get bumped, and they see that wall coming at them. But I'll tell you one thing they *don't* do, Joni. They don't look at that wall! Their natural instincts tell them to, but their training tells them to keep their eyes on the track and steer out of that spin. You see, if they look at the wall, they'll freeze. Your body just reacts; it can't help it. But if you look down the speedway and steer toward that open space, all your nerve endings are concentrating on *that*, not on bracing for an impact."

That's the way we are in our human nature. We fix our eyes on the trial that looms immediately before us, allowing ourselves to become gripped with fear. We say to ourselves, *This is impossible! I'll never get through this. I'll never find a way through. I'll never recover. I'd better brace for an impact, because it's going to be a hard, hard hit. AHHHHHH....*

But after listening to Dan and his race-car wisdom, I realize that the key is to take your eyes off the wall and start concentrating on the future and its opportunities (steer for the open space!), rather than on the present dilemmas that freeze us into impotence.

The apostle Peter was brave to walk on water toward the Lord Jesus, but he too took his focus off the Lord and looked at the wall—and his natural instincts braced for an impact. And what would have happened to the Israelites crossing the Red Sea if they had stood staring, transfixed by the walls of water on each side of them rather than looking ahead of them to the miracle path God had created for them through the heart of the sea?

Little wonder the book of Hebrews tells us to fix our eyes on Jesus, and the author of Colossians says, "Set your heart on things above," and the Gospels say, "Lift up your head, for your salvation draws nigh."

It just may keep you from hitting the wall!

And now, just one last piece of perspective-changing counsel.

Finally ... the Power of a Song

Whenever I'm wheeling through the office, down the hallway, or driving down the freeway, puttering in the backyard, or sitting in the kitchen, I *love* to sing. I wake up in the morning, and my heart wants to sing whenever I'm enjoying the routines of life.

Have you ever wondered if Jesus sang?

In the C. S. Lewis children's book *The Magician's Nephew*, the great lion Aslan sang the world of Narnia into existence. But what does the Bible say of the Son of Man?

I find it quite easy to picture Him singing, humming a melody as He walked up the road from Jericho to Jerusalem. We know that the Jews of that day sang in their synagogues and on their holy feast days. Wouldn't Jesus' family have sung, too? Surely there must have been many times that the Lord's heart filled with joy to overflowing and—you just know He had to let loose with a song.

But does the New Testament actually say so? Does it record any instances of His singing? As a matter of fact, it does. But just one, in Matthew 26:30. The scene for this song, however, is not a sunny hillside.... It's not as He sailed with His disciples in the boat.... It's not as He walked through a vineyard at twilight, the fragrant fruit hanging in great clusters, almost ready to harvest.

It was in the Upper Room on the night Jesus was betrayed. It's recorded that after "they had sung a hymn, they went out to the Mount of Olives" (Matt. 26:30).

It was just before He went to Gethsemane ... and then to the cross.

Of all the times and places, the Lord Jesus chose to have us remember Him singing, it was in the hours before His great sacrifice and death.

This speaks to me in my wheelchair. It shows me how to follow the Lord in song when my heart is heavy, when I'm facing disappointment, when the pain descends, when I'm facing illness or hardship, or when I'm just trying to deal with one more day of paralysis. Ephesians 5:19–20 has some "musical" advice for me. It says, "Sing and make music in your heart to the Lord, always giving thanks to God the Father for everything, in the name of our Lord Jesus Christ."

Did you get that? We are commanded to sing while we always give thanks to God *for everything!* Earlier we read about giving thanks "in" all things, but in this passage, God tells us to always give thanks "for" everything. That little word "for" can encompass an awful lot of pain and suffering. But maybe that's why God reminds us to sing.

The fact is, as you and I follow His steps up the Mount of Olives into the garden of Gethsemane—and down the road to Calvary, too—we also should take up our cross and *sing.* Like this morning when I came to work, I wheeled through the front doors, singing:

> *Happy day, happy day!*
> *When Jesus washed my sins away.*
> *He taught me how to watch and pray,*
> *and live rejoicing every day.*
> *Happy day, happy day!*
> *When Jesus washed my sins away.*[4]

Our natural inclination, of course, is *not* to sing when we're hurting.

But we're not talking about natural inclinations or feelings here; we're talking about singing as an act of faith, trust, and devotion to the Savior who gave Himself for us. (Think of the apostle Paul who sang, despite his chains, in that dungeon in Philippi.)

So my friend, no matter if your emotions are up or down, follow the Lord's lead today. May the mind of Christ your Savior live in you from day to day, and ask God to simply put a song in your heart as you pick up your cross daily and follow Him.

Singing is a perspective changer.

But nothing happens until you open your mouth, by faith, and hit that first note!

EIGHT

ULTIMATE HEALING

When Christ calls me Home I shall go with the
gladness of a boy bounding away from school.
—Adoniram Judson

Through all the years of my paralysis, I have longed—yearned, ached, wept, and prayed—for God's healing in my broken body.

After forty-plus years in my wheelchair, however, I had settled into the realization that in His love, sovereignty, and far-reaching, perfect, but often incomprehensible plan, He has chosen to gently but firmly say, "No, child. Not now. Not yet."

As a result, thoughts of ultimate healing in heaven have frequently become my focus, my passion, my dream, my meditation, and my song. Healing *will* come, and it won't be a halfway job. Restoration to physical wholeness will only be the tiniest fraction of His good plan and purpose for me.

Those thoughts have brought me great peace, even in the face of great trials.

In 1995 I wrote a book on heaven. Meditations on our future, forever home have been one of the principle themes of my ministry, writing, counseling, and speaking ever since.

But when that hostile, disruptive, unwelcome intruder named chronic pain came into my life a couple years ago, it came as a tormentor, mocker, and thief, robbing me of rest, peace, and the ability to do so many of those satisfying and fruitful things God had enabled me to do through the years of quadriplegia. *Paint? Speak? Write? Sing? Travel? Broadcast on radio and TV? Strategic ministry planning?* As of this writing, all of those activities have become infinitely more difficult. Until something changes, I honestly don't know how much longer I will be able to continue them.

All of the old questions about physical healing—some of which I have discussed in this book—have come back to me with a fresh immediacy and flashing-red-light urgency. How can I explain it? It's like thinking you've completed all the requirements and wrapped up a certain college course only to discover that you haven't passed it at all, and that you have a major comprehensive exam immediately in front of you.

I had become "used to" paralysis, if I can put it that way. But I don't know how in the world I can get "used to" constant, driving pain. I had learned how to cope with the hassles, hardships, and seemingly endless physical necessities and routines of quadriplegia, but I don't know how to cope with nonstop agony. *I need rescuing. I need deliverance. I need healing from this suffering. I need God to do something. As quickly as possible.*

I used to dial His number at various times throughout the daylight and nighttime hours; now it's a moment by moment 911 call to God—on speed dial.

I used to pray for grace to maximize each day; now I pray for survival.

"Quickly Psalms"

As a result of these unwanted changes in my life, I have become a great fan of what I call the "Quickly Psalms." These are those psalms—mostly David's—in which he not only makes his requests of God, but adds a "rush order" to them. In other words, "Lord, I'm making this request (and I know I need to wait on You), but I really don't have a lot of leisure time to wait on Your answer. If You don't come through pretty quickly, then You don't have to bother with answering at all, because I will be toast!"

Just listen to the sheer urgency of these ancient cries for help, from the psalm:

> But you, O LORD, be not far off;
>> *O my Strength, come quickly to help me....*

> Turn your ear to me,
>> *come quickly to my rescue....*

> *Come quickly to help me,*
>> O Lord my Savior....

> Be pleased, O Lord, to save me;
>> *O Lord, come quickly to help me....*

> Do not hide your face from your servant;
>> *answer me quickly, for I am in trouble.*
> Come near and rescue me....

> Hasten, O God, to save me;
>> *O Lord, come quickly to help me....*

> Yet I am poor and needy;
>> *come quickly to me, O God.*
> You are my help and my deliverer;
>> O Lord, do not delay....

Be not far from me, O God;
　　come quickly, O my God, to help me....

May your mercy come quickly to meet us,
　　for we are in desperate need....

Do not hide your face from me
　　when I am in distress.
Turn your ear to me;
　　when I call, answer me quickly....

O Lord, I call to you; come quickly to me.
　　Hear my voice when I call to you....

Answer me quickly, O Lord;
　　my spirit fails.[1]

You gotta love it. David is saying, "Oh, won't You hurry, Lord? Yes, I honor You for Your grace, Your provision, Your compassion, and Your deliverance. But is there any way You could maybe grease the skids just a little? Maybe send the help by FedEx priority overnight instead of by mule train?"

I like that. I like the fact that the Bible acknowledges that we will find ourselves in emergencies and times of deep distress or intense fear when we need immediate help or an emergency injection of hope directly into a main artery of our soul.

When Peter found the sea surface on which he walked suddenly more liquid than a few moments before, he uttered what may be the shortest prayer in the Bible:

But when he saw the wind, he was afraid and,

beginning to sink, cried out, "Lord, save me!"
(Matt. 14:30)

So yes, I've been uttering some Peter Prayers and Quickly Psalms of my own. My prayers for healing have come back to an urgent level—more reminiscent of those times when I was a scared teenager in a Baltimore hospital than at any time in many, many years.

But this present life crisis has had another effect as well.

It has trebled my heart's longing for the ultimate healing that will be mine just around the corner in heaven. My friend, this is not a daydream or a pleasant diversion for me; it's a lifeline. It's hope. It's sanity. It's a place where my mind can go when it's way too difficult to contemplate where I am.

A death wish?

Not at all. It's a simple longing for the comfort, relief, refreshment, and joy of my Father's house. I already have a room with my name on it, paid for, reserved, and waiting for me; *Jesus told me so.*

> There is plenty of room for you in my Father's
> home. If that weren't so, would I have told you
> that I'm on my way to get a room ready for you?
> And if I'm on my way to get your room ready, I'll
> come back and get you so you can live where I
> live. (John 14:2–3 MSG)

Does that still sound morbid to you? It shouldn't.

Let me illustrate. I have friends who backpack and have described the experience to me. Now just imagine a fifty-five-pound pack on your back—the straps digging into your shoulder muscles—and a long, long hike with zigzagging switchbacks and a steep elevation gain. Now imagine that you're on the return journey, back to the trailhead, your car, and home. The sun burns down on you, you stub your toes on roots and rocks, you're covered with dust, scratches, and mosquito bites, your shoulders ache, your legs are beginning to feel like rubber, and you know from the small fires within your hiking boots that your blisters are making a serious statement.

Sure, you may still share some good conversation with your hiking buddies. You may still be walking through some spectacular terrain—with mountain views at every corner, wildlife in the forest glades, puffy cumulus clouds riding through a blue vault of sky, and lovely trickling streams winding through alpine meadows. It's all very nice and pleasing to the eye, and part of your soul acknowledges every scene of beauty and gives thanks to a mighty Creator.

But mostly, you just want to go home.

You can't wait to take the pack off your shoulders, the boots off your smoldering feet, get out of that sun that saps your energy, take a long, long drink of something cold, climb into a hot, soapy shower, and start telling your loved ones about your journey.

It's the longing of the saints in the book of Hebrews:

> These men of faith I have mentioned died without ever receiving all that God had promised them; but they saw it all awaiting them on ahead and were glad, for they agreed that this earth was not their real home but that they were just strangers visiting down here. And quite obviously when they talked like that, they were looking forward to their real home in heaven.
>
> If they had wanted to, they could have gone back to the good things of this world. But they didn't want to. They were living for heaven. And now

> God is not ashamed to be called their God, for
> he has made a heavenly city for them. (Heb.
> 11:13–16 TLB)

These good people, weary and worn from long journeys, saw a city sparkling on the far horizon, and knew it for what is was: *home*. The only home they really desired. And they were filled with longing and pangs of homesickness for a place where they had never seen, but a place where they truly belonged.

"Happily Ever After"

All of us have special books that have been handed down to us, and I'm no exception. I'm thinking of a big red book of fairy tales that sat on a shelf in my sister's bedroom. It had beautiful end pages, and each story was illustrated with lots of detail.

To this day, if you were to ask me what the Pied Piper looked like, I could give you an exact description—all the way down to his funny hat and pointed shoes. Even when I see twisted oak trees, I think of the color plates in that big red book of fairy tales.

And oh, what wonderful memories! I can close my eyes and hear Daddy coming upstairs in the evening to help us girls get settled in. He'd open up that book and read to Kathy and me. Hansel and Gretel … Goldilocks and the Three Bears … Little Red Riding Hood … Billy Goats Gruff. (Does anyone ever read these stories to children anymore?) They were classic stories of good and evil, and the best part was always near the end of the story.

My father's voice would slow a little as he read those final, heartwarming words: "And they lived happily ever after." It meant Hansel and Gretel lived, and the old witch died, Little Red Riding Hood survived, and the nasty old wolf was banished. The goats had the run of the pasture, and the old troll was never seen again. It's wonderful to live happily ever after.

No matter how young a child is—no matter what he believes about God and heaven—every boy and girl instinctively knows what "happily ever after" means. You don't have to teach them about it. Children seem to know, they realize that this world is full of wolves, trolls, and big bad bears. They're aware that things aren't quite right, that something's wrong with the world, and we all want—we long—for that time when we will live happily ever after. When the prince will finally kiss us and we will wake up from this strange dream and enter true happiness and joy forever and ever.

Sounds rather biblical, doesn't it?

That's because it is.

The book of Ecclesiastes says that God has put eternity in the heart of man. We can't exactly put our finger on it, but it's there, all right. This itchy longing for eternity … this wanting everything to be "okay" … to live happily ever after.

That's why faith in Jesus Christ is so satisfying, so fulfilling. For only in Christ is every longing fulfilled, every hope realized, every yearning for peace and well-being finally answered. In Christ is the culmination of that classic struggle and the defeat of all things evil, when our wonderful Savior will right every wrong, and the Prince of Peace will be our King of Kings.

There is a happy ending ahead. I can almost hear His footsteps on the stairs. Jesus, come quickly!

Conflicted?

Am I conflicted when I consider these things? *Of course* I am. How could it be otherwise for any of us? We have a temporary address here on this broken planet, but we're told beyond doubt that we are citizens of another place. Not only that, but the true essence of who we are is actually seated or settled in heaven with Christ already, as it says in Colossians 3:1.

So yes, I am torn.

On one hand I want to go be with the Lord Jesus—no buts about it. I want Him to close the door on Satan and suffering. No more death, no more pain, no more sorrow, no more wheelchair, no more braces, no more leg bags. And when I read the Bible, I see tons of verses that encourage us to fix our hearts and minds on heavenly glories above. I come across verses all the time that speak about how good it is to *long* for Christ's return and for heaven's arrival.

But then! Then we come across almost as many verses that tell us to roll up our sleeves and work hard here on earth. Put your hand to the plow.... ... Work, for the night is coming.... Invest your talents. And even though the apostle Paul himself desired deeply to be in heaven, he thinks twice, then says to his friends at church, "It is better that I remain." He goes on to say, "Work out your salvation with fear and trembling. Sow seeds, shake salt, shine light, make fishers of men, spread the good news, travel to the uttermost parts of the earth. Hey: We've got *work* to do! The gospel's got to get out there."

The truth is, the Bible communicates both messages at the same time. And where it concerns heaven? *That* is where I feel the conflict. Like the apostle, I deeply, profoundly desire to go to be with Jesus. Yet on the other hand, lots of my friends, relatives, and folks in my community don't know Christ. So I've got to keep my hand to the plow and work and sow seeds and shine light and not let up!

But does that mean I am not to long for the Lord's return as urgently?

I was talking about this with my girlfriend this morning. I was telling her about the many people I know who aren't saved. We were talking about the day-to-day labor (sometimes very heavy labor) of plowing furrows in God's vineyard and rightfully reclaiming earth as the Lord's. I explained to her that sometimes I feel a little conflicted that I mustn't long too deeply or too much for heaven, because there's so much work on earth to do.

Her answer?

She quoted Revelation 22:20 (KJV): "Even so, come, Lord Jesus."

I looked at my friend kind of funny and then she explained. "Maybe that's why it says 'even so.'"

It was like a light flicked on in my mind. Yes, there's work to do here on earth, but I don't need to think I'm longing too much for heaven, because the Bible says "even so." In other words, *even though* there's lots of work, many to win, and much to accomplish, even in light of all those things, we are to long with all of our hearts and say "come, Lord Jesus."

And I would add "come quickly." (There's that *quickly* word again!)

I'd like to leave you with four simple meditations on heaven from a backpacker who has it in her sights and can't wait to take that last step off the path, emerge at trail's end, let the pack slide from my shoulders, and step into the embrace of my Savior—be it today, tomorrow, next week, or twenty years from now.

Meditation No. 1: Too Easily Pleased?

The good things in this life are only glimpses of what lies ahead for God's sons and daughters. The trouble is we get so caught up in the here and now that we end up being far too satisfied with the good things down on earth. We tend to forget about the better things yet to come.

C. S. Lewis has said that if we consider the unblushing promises of reward held forth in the Gospels,

> It would seem that our Lord finds our desires not too strong but too weak. We are half-hearted creatures, fooling around … when infinite joy is offered to us. Like an ignorant child who wants to go on making mud pies in a slum because he cannot imagine what is meant by the offer of a holiday at the seashore. We are too easily pleased.

We *are* too easily pleased. It's true from the time that we are children—and I can illustrate from my own experience.

Growing up in Baltimore, Maryland, the very idea of going to the mountains thrilled me. When I was young, my mom and dad announced to the family that we were about to take a trip to the Rocky Mountains. *Mountains.* That's all I needed to hear. I got so excited about the idea of rock climbing. I'd always heard about the marvelous views from those big peaks. And I taxed my imagination to the limit trying to picture what it would be like to drive in the car and look straight up at the cliffs that reach the sky.

When we began our trip it took us only a day or two to arrive at the Appalachian Mountains. We stopped at lots of viewpoints, and I was thrilled at the chance to climb the hillsides. Everything looked so big and wide open—I couldn't imagine a place more beautiful.

Bottom line: I didn't want to go on. Why should we? I wanted to stay. I was far too easily pleased.

Continuing our journey, we descended out of the Appalachians and onto the flat plains of the Midwest. I was convinced my parents made a wrong turn. Let's go back to the Appalachians! Who wants the Rockies? All I could see for miles around was flat as the proverbial pancake.

Ah, but I can remember the thrill to this day, seeing those magnificent Rockies rise up out of nowhere. Mountains like I'd never dreamed of before. I forgot all about the Appalachians.

Yes, we humans—so enraptured with the present, the here and now, so caught up with the things we can touch and feel and see—are far too easily pleased.

For some of us, we've just got to quit making mud pies down here on earth. A holiday at the seashore has been offered to us. A trip to mountains higher and more majestic than we could ever dream. And we had better realize—and start living as if—the good things on earth are only mere glimpses of marvelously better things just ahead.

Meditation No. 2: The Best of the Best

How would you describe heaven to someone who has never heard about it or read about it in God's Word?

Sometimes when I want to paint a picture of what heaven will be like—especially for those who don't believe in God—I borrow the words of the prophet Isaiah, letting him set the scene.

> On this mountain the LORD Almighty will prepare
> a feast of rich food for all peoples,
> a banquet of aged wine—
> the best of meats and the finest of wines.
> (Isa. 25:6)

When I have read that verse from the Bible to people—particularly non-Christians—they look at me and say, "Huh?" Never in their lives have they heard such a thing. Their idea of heaven was a bunch of ghostly looking saints sitting around on clouds surrounded by angels plucking harps. They never thought heaven could be so … earthy.

Or is it heavenly?

The point Isaiah is trying to make is that heaven is rock-solid *real*. Much more real than anything we can see, touch, or taste on this earth.

It's not just meat, it's the *best* of meats.

It's not just wine, it's the *finest* of wines.

Everything will be far better than anything we ever experienced on earth. I tell these unbelievers, "The most beautiful, pleasurable things one could enjoy here on this planet are only hints and whispers, and omens—mere crayon scribbles on a grocery sack—of even greater, more glorious things. Pleasures on earth are just shadows of their *realities* in heaven.

And then I say, "I will sit down at the wedding supper of the Lord with Moses, toasting Martin Luther and King David, and giving a hug to the prophet Daniel. And I'll look up and there walking toward me will be my dad and mother, and before you know it, we'll break up into laughter and we will wipe our eyes and try to stop, then start laughing again, saying, 'We're here … they're here … you're here!' And Jesus Christ will open our eyes to the great fountain of love in His heart for us, beyond all that we ever experienced on earth … and when we finally stop laughing and crying, Jesus Himself really will wipe away every one of our tears. That's right, *every* one"(Rev. 21:4).

Then I will say to these unbelievers, "Are you prepared for heaven? Are you ready to meet your Maker? It's a holy place for holy inhabitants. May I explain how you can get ready?"

Heaven's coming, and it's real.

And I really want you—and all my friends—to be there.

Meditation No. 3: Sown in Dishonor … Raised in Honor

There is a special ring that's been passed down in our family. It is a beautiful, antique-cut diamond ring in a platinum setting. I possessed it for awhile a few years ago, but then went ahead and passed it on to my niece, Jayme Kay.

It's a stunning ring—a full-karat diamond. But if you look closely, way down deep inside the translucent stone, you'll see a tiny speck of black carbon in the stone. Now I realize it's just a minor flaw, but it reminds me of where that diamond came from—its beginnings.

Diamonds, of course, are the hardest naturally forming material on the planet, renowned for strength, durability, and stunning beauty. The precious stone's name is drawn from *adamas*, the Greek word for "invincible."

Formed by incredible pressure and mind-boggling temperatures deep within the earth's mantle, a diamond begins life as carbon deep inside the earth. Once mined, rough diamonds are sorted into thousands of categories according to shape, quality, and color. No two diamonds in the entire world are the same.

Every single diamond, however, begins as black carbon that eventually turns into a precious, stunning gem. Sown in dishonor, it's something akin to black coal. Raised in honor, carbon can become a highly valuable gemstone. It's an illustration that always makes me think of 1 Corinthians 15:42–44:

> So will it be with the resurrection of the dead. The body that is sown is perishable, it is raised imperishable; it is sown in dishonor, it is raised in glory; it is sown in weakness, it is raised in power; it is sown a natural body, it is raised a spiritual body.

What a lesson a little bit of carbon can teach us, for it serves as a model of how awesome, wondrous, and incalculably different—yet very much the same—our glorified body in heaven will be from our earthly body. Heaven is going to be so unspeakably glorious, and we will be as different and far better from what we are now as a diamond is different and far, far better than a piece of primordial black rock.

I like to meditate on that as I sit here in this wheelchair of mine. My body wasn't all that great when I was on my feet many years ago, but it's even worse now—what with atrophied muscles, misshapen hands and fingers, and deteriorating bones with their attendant agonies.

Now you have to understand that for me, just to have a body like yours that actually *works* … well, that would be fantastic. I would feel as if I were already in heaven if I could but run and walk and hold things with my hands. But the marvelous truth about 1 Corinthians 15 is that in heaven I won't just get back my earthly body that functions in all the expected earthly ways. No, it will be a glorified body that will suit me perfectly for both the new heaven and the new earth.

I think it's interesting that a diamond is, in its very essence, the same thing as carbon. The only difference is in how time and pressure create an entirely new substance. (Although, as I said, it is one and the same as the black lump of dirty stuff from which it came.) In the same way, my friend, my heavenly body will be a new and improved version of this old one in which I now reside. The only difference is how time and pressure (a lot of pressure) will change this earthly garment into something so bright, so precious, so perfect, so multifaceted, that it will shine like a star in the night sky.

Meditation No. 4: Ultimate Fulfillment

Sitting in a wheelchair for over four decades has loaded me with a lifetime of memories of what it was like to be on my feet—everything from feeling my fingers on the cool keys of a piano to diving through the breakers at high tide to peeling an orange to holding the hand of someone I love.

These memories flood every nerve and fiber of my being … and ignite my imagination. Whatever it is I have lost here on earth, whether it be the ability to hold things or feel things, or to run or to walk—whatever it is I have lost, it will all be regained in heaven. And not just "regained"! Even the best memories of walking and running and swimming and riding a horse—why, these are whispers and faded newspaper images of how much *more* I will have in heaven.

And our relationship with our Savior? Oh, it will be much, much more. It had better be! Because the whisper of every good thing on earth will find completeness and fulfillment in heaven. I will do so much more than peel an orange or touch a flower or run across a meadow. Those are good things and treasured memories. But they are only hints and promises of more wonderful things yet to be fulfilled. Yes, I certainly love the Lord Jesus on earth. But in heaven? In His physical presence? Wow. I will love

Him as purely and perfectly and as completely as He loves me. I can't even begin to imagine how wonderful that will be, but the Bible promises me that one day in heaven, the earthly Joni will step into the glorious Joni God intended me to be.

The best thing about heaven will not be running or walking, touching or holding. The best thing about heaven will be a pure heart no longer weighed down by sin and selfishness. And I can say *that* from this wheelchair. Glorified bodies? Hey, bring it on. But a pure, glorified heart? *That's* the best!

A Dream of Heaven

I dreamed of heaven the other night.

In the dream I was on my feet, not in a wheelchair. I don't have those sorts of dreams often, but when I do, it's a delight.

Actually, I had been reading the book of Revelation, the part about God wiping away our tears. I had been thinking about the marvelous thought that, one day, it will be God's responsibility—not my friends', not my husband's, not the angels', it won't even be my responsibility—and pleasure to wipe away my tears.

Anyway, in this dream I was sitting at my old piano—the same old black baby grand piano in my parents' living room. Before my paralyzing accident I had taken ten years of piano lessons on that old thing. Unlike some kids who hate taking piano lessons, I loved it.

In my dream I couldn't see myself sitting on the piano bench; all I could see were my hands. I was watching myself playing a piece by Schumann, a favorite of mine called "Romanze." It is the loveliest piece he composed for the piano. And here's what was amazing: I knew that as I was playing, it had been years since my accident. And I wondered as I was sitting there watching myself play, *How am I able to remember this? It's been ages since I played this thing!*

But the miracle in my dream was that my hands and fingers had memorized all the movements on the keys, all the chords, all the runs, where one bar of music led to the next. My fingers knew it all, and I just sat there, playing and smiling. I can't tell you how delightful it was.

I woke up astounded and I wondered immediately if, in fact, those were the correct notes and chords for that piece in my dream. Somehow, I wouldn't put it past my brain to remember it all. It's a little like memorizing Scripture, isn't it? Or maybe an old hymn. You commit it to memory, practice it by heart, over and over, and just when you think you've forgotten it, it pops up.

Oh friend, heaven will be wonderful. The sights, the sounds, the people, the things we'll do, the places we'll explore, the friends we'll make, the kingdom we'll rule, the fun things we'll learn, the joy of being with our God, the happy-hearted praise we'll give our Savior, the angels, the heavenly hosts. And music? Just imagine following the river of music to its very source, the very headwaters, where it bubbles up out the bedrock of heaven in an artesian fountain!

Yes, I dreamed a dream, then woke up back here on earth with all the pain and pressure of another day.

It reminds me of a story someone told me about a man on his deathbed. His pastor had been sitting with him, holding his hand, keeping him company. The dying man had fallen asleep for a moment, and when he opened his eyes, he said, "Is that you, pastor?"

"Yes, it's me," the minster answered. "I'm still here with you."

"Oh," the man moaned. "I'm so disappointed! I thought I was going to see Jesus, and it's just you!"

Soon, however, the man slipped away from his earthly life. And we can have no doubt at all that when he opened his eyes that next time, he wasn't disappointed at all.

Far from it!

NINE

SUFFERING ... AND THE HARVEST

Those who sow tears shall reap joy. Yes, they
go out weeping, carrying seed for sowing, and
return singing, carrying their sheaves.
Psalm 126:5–6 TLB

I began this book by describing this particular season of my life as one of all-out warfare with virtually nonstop pain.

I've certainly fought many battles through the years on many different fronts. But in God's wisdom and sovereign timing, He has chosen to allow this era of my life, near my sixtieth year, as a time when the war has become unusually intense.

Maybe that's where you are in life today. Against your inclination and every desire, you've had to become a fighter. It could be a fight for your marriage, a struggle over employment or finances, a long-running custody battle, or an arm-wrestling match with the bureaucracy over adopting a child. Maybe you have a special-needs child, and every day seems like a mighty struggle to just keep your head above water. Or perhaps, like me, you had to climb into the ring for the thousandth round with energy-sapping, mind-scrambling pain.

No one *wants* a personal war, and everyone who has one would like to be rid of it. But in Christ, however, the hardships themselves *are not wasted*. As tools in the hands of a loving, all-wise, sovereign God, these very struggles that cause us such frustration, sadness, anxiety, and tears, will bring back benefits to our lives a thousandfold.

Did I say a thousandfold? The apostle Paul would scorn such a number, asserting that it's ridiculous to even try to do comparisons. He wrote, "In my opinion whatever we may have to go through now is less than nothing compared with the magnificent future God has in store for us."[1] The writer to the Hebrews reminds us that our current hardship, if we endure it as loving discipline, will produce "a harvest of righteousness and peace for those who have been trained by it."[2]

For me, the pain has been great ... but *so has the harvest*.

Among other things, my personal conflict has this undeniable benefit: It is a vivid reminder to me of the ceaseless warfare between the kingdom of darkness and the kingdom of light, all across our world at this very moment.

Sometimes, when our days are comfortable and easy, when we're wrapped in the warm web of family and friends and activities and abundance, we can forget one of the most basic realities in all of life: that we are members of a great worldwide body in which much suffering is occurring.

Some people use electronic devices to remind themselves of events and appointments in their lives—cell phones and iPhones and PDAs that chirp, bleat, tweet, or startle everyone with loud clips of dance music.

Physical pain is a reminder, too.

It's a sharp, unrelenting prod to remember that many men, women, and little ones who belong to our Lord Jesus are—right this moment—also wrestling with pain

—or contending with dark, hateful powers that seek to crush them.

—or fighting for life itself.

For years now I've had what you might call an "enforced opportunity" to pray for people and needs and ministries in just about every corner of the planet. Because of my condition, I have to be put in my bed early every evening, with hours remaining before I'm ready for sleep.

On many such nights, I've used those hours to plug into a matchless worldwide network—and it's not CNN, Fox News, the BBC, or the Home and Garden channel. I simply begin to pray for fellow believers in multiple nations that I'm aware of, or have come to know through the years, who find themselves on the ragged edge of poverty, pain, oppression, or need—or those who have devoted their days to working with these dear souls.

When you watch CNN, you get to observe and hear the stories—tales of woe—about people enduring all manner of natural and man-made heartaches, disasters, and tragedies. But when you turn off the TV and begin to *intercede* before the throne of God for saints scattered like diamond dust across the map of the world, you actually find yourself becoming part of the story! And you have the privilege of seeing those sad stories change, as God steps in with grace, provision, courage, perseverance, hope, and yes, sometimes miraculous healing.

Some people I will pray for now and then, on a rotating basis week by week. Others, like my Pain Pal, I pray for every day.

Africa: My Pain Pal

> *Sometimes I feel discouraged and think my work's*
> *in vain,*
> *But then the Holy Spirit revives my soul again.*
> *There is a balm in Gilead to make the wounded*
> *whole;*
> *There is a balm in Gilead to heal the sin-sick soul.*

I sing this African American spiritual a lot when I'm feeling discouraged or filled with fear and doubt. I sing it when I'm fighting off anxiety or worry, wondering if my disability will get worse. Songs like these are an encouragement to me; and I'm glad the Lord has given me "songs in the night," as the Bible puts it.

But God has also given me something else to encourage me when my wheelchair begins to get me down. It's a photograph hanging next to my desk where I work. I don't know the name of the man in the photo, and I'm not even sure what town he lives in. But he is my inspiration.

Let me tell you why: Our Wheels for the World team members met this man, lying outside his little house, during one of our wheelchair distributions in Africa. His "house" was little more than a roofless lean-to, made up of cinder blocks and banana leaves. When our team members encountered him, he was lying against half of a trashcan, with his back propped against the wall—apparently the only position that gave him a measure of comfort.

The villagers all knew he was in great and constant pain. He's a Christian, and his church helps meet some of his needs; others give him alcohol to deaden the pain. Day after day he lies there. It's all that he *can* do.

When my friend on the Wheels team asked if he could take a photo, the man said, "Wait," and slowly pulled his drooping shirt up over his shoulder. "Now it's okay," he said. This man in deep pain still possessed a sense of human dignity. And no, he didn't want a wheelchair. What good would it do? It would hurt too much to try to use one. He just wanted us to pray for him.

And so I do. Every day.

Romans 12:4 says that each member of the body of Christ belongs to the other. That is a powerful statement … and worth a moment's meditation. Because God tells me in His Word that I am intimately connected with that man in pain. He belongs to me, and I belong to him. My victory in pain— somehow, some way—helps him. And it's why I keep his photograph above my desk. His battle is my battle, and my battle is also his.

People who walk into my office sometimes ask about this African man in the photo. Well, I can't say his name; I may never learn it this side of heaven. But I can tell his story. And if ever I start to feel a little sorry for myself, I just look up and remind myself that he is the body of Christ ... and so am I. And each member of the body belongs to the other.

Maybe you haven't thought much about Romans 12:4 and your larger family scattered across the nations. Maybe it hasn't occurred to you for awhile that you have *real* brothers and sisters with needs and hopes and dreams and sorrows who walk with the same Jesus that you walk with every day.

I'd like this little chapter to just remind you when you find yourself wrestling with hard times, financial shortfalls, or maybe severe pain, that your family suffers those things too—and seeks provision from their Lord. Remember the words of Peter?

> Take a firm stand against him, and be strong in
> your faith. Remember that your Christian brothers
> and sisters all over the world are going through the
> same kind of suffering you are. (1 Peter 5:9 NLT)

In the next few pages, come meet some very special members of your family in faraway places. And let me just add this: I would have never met these believers, or had the opportunity to help them, apart from my disability and my wheelchair.

From Cuba: Healing After Forty-Seven Years

Jesús is a forty-seven-year-old Cuban man who is not only paralyzed, but has some brain damage, too. His father brought him to our wheelchair distribution that October 22, which just happened to be Jesús' birthday. A new wheelchair and Bible were two birthday gifts everyone in the family would always remember. While Jesús was being fitted for his chair, his dad told us what happened on the day their son was born.

It was 1962, during what has become known in the history books as the first day the public became aware of the Cuban Missile Crisis. On that day, our whole nation went on red alert, President Kennedy went on TV, and Americans everywhere braced themselves for an all-out Soviet nuclear attack launched from Cuba. In later years, Soviet general and army chief of operations Anatoly Gribkov wrote that "Nuclear catastrophe was hanging by a thread … and we weren't counting days or hours, but minutes."

As frightening as October 22, 1962, might have been in America, the residents of Cuba were also terrified. They had been told that the Americans were going to bomb *them*. The Castro government put out an alert, and there was a mad rush to evacuate many buildings, including hospitals. At that very unhappy moment in Havana, Jesús was being born. All the nurses had to leave the floor, but the soon-to-be mother just couldn't leave. She had to deliver her own baby with no one to assist. In the process, her tiny infant fell to the floor and landed on his head—causing permanent brain damage. You can imagine the hurt and resentment Jesús' mother and father harbored against America ever since then.

But there we were, over forty-six years later—fifteen of us Americans—presenting Jesús and his mother and father with a new wheelchair, as well as the life-changing gospel of Jesus Christ. And that gospel brought healing, help, and hope to this little Cuban family. Jesús was so excited. His father, in tears, said to us, "Now I will be able to take my son outside for walks in his wheelchair."

You know … a nuclear disaster was not only averted years ago in October, a disaster of another sort was averted in that this family was rescued out of spiritual darkness. Psalm 57:1 says, "Have mercy on me, O God…. I will take refuge in the shadow of your wings until the disaster has passed."

Do you see what I mean? That's just one little story that would have never happened, apart from my diving accident, my paralysis, God's repeated no to my requests for immediate healing, and the eventual ministries we began that became known as Joni and Friends and Wheels for the World.

Out of the hardship, out of the suffering, a harvest of righteousness and peace, and eternal life for a Cuban family that had known so much bitterness and sorrow.

Now you may be reading these words about our Cuba team and perhaps thinking that you wouldn't be very comfortable doing what they do—leaving your familiar safety zone to bring help to impoverished people in spiritually dark and sometimes dangerous places. Yes, in fact it can be a risky proposition sometimes. And if you decided to never participate in such an outreach, you could avoid some of those risks.

But you might also miss some very unique gifts you could find nowhere else in life.

From Cameroon: Joyceline's Song

I have a physical-therapist friend who recently received the most priceless, precious gift you can imagine.

But it wasn't a normal gift. Not at all.

My friend arrived in Cameroon, a very poor country on the west coast of Africa, with our team, ready to go and fit disabled children to new wheelchairs.

It turned out to be very difficult for the team to travel to the place where we were to distribute the chairs. It took six hours by jeep on steep, rutted roads, and it took the truck loaded with hundreds of wheelchairs even longer than that. Hours later, it was pitch-dark by the time they pulled up to the small center where all the people with disabilities were.

They'd been arriving all afternoon from distant villages, literally dragging themselves through the dirt, or being carried by relatives. Now the little center—even this late at night—was packed full of disabled people resting on the floor in thin blankets.

Even so, they were deliriously happy when our physical therapists pulled up outside. Our team kept the lights of the jeep and the truck turned on, while disabled children and adults and family members spilled out of the door into the parking area, where they celebrated the team's arrival with a welcome song. They were so excited that their song lasted over an hour!

The next morning our team began fitting each disabled child and adult. There was one little girl named Joyceline who had an enlarged head due to hydrocephalus; she was not able to walk and had also been battling malaria. She was the quiet one who watched all the goings on, sitting silently on the floor with a shy smile, wide-open eyes not missing a thing.

She waited her turn without complaining or whining. Finally, when several hours went by, it was time to fit Joyceline.

And that's where the unusual gift comes in.

As my physical therapist friend started measuring this precious African child, the little girl began singing (almost in a whisper) a song over the physical therapist. She placed her tiny hand on my friend's shoulder, and began composing her own little worship song.

> *Jesus loves our friends, and He cares so much for us.*
>
> *He loves you for helping us, and sharing with us*
> *His care.*
>
> *Jesus is the One we love so much; we are happy in*
> *His love.*
>
> *We want to say we love you too.*

Joyceline made up that little song as she went along, singing her praise and worship to God while she rested her little hand on the physical therapist's shoulder. (Our charismatic friends might say she was "singing in the Spirit.")

That day the Spirit of Christ permeated the entire hillside of that small village in Cameroon, and our Wheels team members discovered that those who are poor in this world are often the richest in faith. Not only that, the physical therapist received the best gift ever—the gratitude of this dear little daughter of the living God.

Oh sure, she had given Joyceline the gift of a wheelchair. But what my friend received was far more valuable. Really, priceless: the incalculable thankfulness of the poorest of the poor.

I still look at Joyceline's photo from time to time, with her bright smile and shiny eyes. A picture of the joy of Jesus ... flowing straight out of suffering.

From Uganda: Lazarus, Come Forth!

The final day of our wheelchair and Bible distribution was held in a mud-and-stick house in a small village called Nyarushanje.

Mrs. Dimbirwe brought her husband, Semu, for a wheelchair. Some years earlier he had fallen from a tree, breaking his right leg and hip, and incurring a severe brain injury. His chin was on his chest, sitting there on the floor silent, almost catatonic. It was as if everyone around him didn't exist; he sat there shrunken and frozen.

No one talked to Semu, not even his wife. In fact, no one ever talked to him. But while they were waiting for his wheelchair, one of our team members, Dana Croxton, began explaining to Mrs. Dimbirwe how important it is to keep up communication with a brain-injured person.

Lifting Semu's head, Dana began to ask him to perform a few tasks—simple things like squeezing Dana's hand or resisting a push.

Then the Holy Spirit broke in with something that wasn't a part of the normal therapist-patient interaction. Dana began to speak directly to Semu, telling him he was a man like anyone else, an equal and a brother, that God loved him and Jesus died for him, and that God wasn't angry over this injury, but deeply valued Semu.

This went on for about two minutes. Those looking on must have thought Dana had lost his senses, because there was no visible response from the disabled man.

And then, very suddenly, Semu came to life.

In an instant, the injured man became very animated, smiling, laughing, and then speaking in a firm voice back to Dana. Soon the two men were weeping and hugging as Semu firmly squeezed both of Dana's hands.

Finally, just before Dana began the wheelchair fitting, Semu reached up and pulled Dana to hug him. Hard. He then said into Dana's ear in perfect English, "You are my brother, my friend, and God loves me."

Everyone was stunned and amazed—and no one more so than Semu's wife. Just moments earlier he had sat there shriveled and silent, with no one relating to him. And it was probably because no one really believed there was "anybody" inside that shell of a man.

John chapter 11 gives us the account of Jesus and Lazarus. It's a hair-raising, soul-stirring moment when Jesus calls forth a dead man, saying, "Come out!" And you know the story from there. Lazarus walks out of his grave to the utter amazement of everyone.

Well, that day in the small village of Nyarushanje, Uganda, a man named Semu, with severe disabilities—and probably in great pain—came forth from a living grave. It may not have been physical death from which he emerged, as Lazarus did centuries earlier, but most assuredly, a man was called out of spiritual death to life by the Son of God Himself.

The miracle took place because a member of our team took the time to not only notice him, but with his compassionate touch and words of kindness, he inasmuch as told Semu, "Come out!"

Dana reached out and treated him with respect and dignity, knowing full well that, yes, there truly was somebody inside that physical shell—a man greatly loved by Jesus.

From Peru: The Little Red Wheelchair

It's always hard to let go when your child goes to be with the Lord. After all, it's not supposed to be that way; children are supposed to bury their parents, not the other way around.

That's how Kim and Jay felt when their eight-year-old daughter, Lindy, with cerebral palsy, went home to be with Jesus after a bad seizure in 1998.

All they had left was Lindy's little wheelchair. It was a red one with a seatbelt and shoulder and foot straps that supported their girl so well on her school-bus rides down the rutted dirt roads of Alaska, with so many potholes.

Jay and Kim had something else left, too, in the wake of their daughter's departure: They had a deep desire to honor little Lindy by personally taking her small wheelchair on a Wheels for the World trip in order to give it to another disabled child.

That's how Jay and Kim ended up going with our Peru team a few years after Lindy's passing. As they were flying to South America, frequently praying together, they wondered just who would be receiving Lindy's little red wheelchair.

At that same time, another mother and father were wondering about a wheelchair. Gladys and Ruben Suarez lived in the little village of Pichus up in the Sierra Mountains eighty miles east of Lima, with their six children. Because their eleven-year-old, Christian, was afflicted with cerebral palsy and couldn't walk or even crawl, his parents had to carry him wherever he needed to go.

Without a wheelchair, Christian had never had the opportunity to attend school. *This* is what Gladys and Ruben had been praying about—something that seemed almost impossible to them. They needed a child-sized wheelchair—one with side supports and shoulder and foot straps—the kind of wheelchair that Christian could use on the rutted dirt roads around their village, roads with so many potholes.

Little wonder that on the day our team arrived in downtown Lima for distribution, Gladys and Ruben had thought nothing of traveling by bus for four hours with little Christian on their lap. They were traveling with high hopes ... as were Jay and Kim from faraway Alaska. Neither at that time knew that within hours, their hopes would be realized. A little red wheelchair with shoulder straps and foot straps would find a home. Amid smiles and songs, the families would meet, a spark would ignite, and—superseding any language barrier—there would be laughter and tears.

It would be easy to imagine the Lord Jesus looking on, perhaps with His arm around little Lindy.

Remember that "network" I mentioned earlier in the chapter?

Remember how I said that God doesn't waste our pain?

In His good pleasure, He brought two families, half a world apart, together in His name. The surface details of language and culture that divided them were nothing compared to the living, eternal bonds that grafted their lives: love of family, love of Jesus, patience in suffering, and membership in a worldwide body that enables them to experience each other's pain ... and be lifted by each other's joy.

From Peru: A Mother's Prayer

In the town of Arequipa, Peru, on the next-to-the-last day of the distribution, all the child-sized wheelchairs had been distributed. All the team had left was one pediatric wheelchair that was so wide it was virtually unusable. The team put it aside because it wasn't suitable for any disabled boys or girls.

Just about that time a woman from the mountains arrived with her little disabled girl, Claudia, wrapped in a blanket on her back. The journey had been long and difficult, and she was afraid—you could see it in her face—that she was too late.

And truthfully, she was too late.

There were no more pediatric wheelchairs left.

Claudia's mother, however, had come too far with hopes too high to simply turn away and go home empty-handed. Instead, she sat outside the distribution center all afternoon and *prayed*. It broke our hearts to see her out there, with little Claudia in her lap, waiting on the Lord for what she could never provide herself. And there simply weren't any more wheelchairs to be had! What could they possibly do for her?

That night Samuel, one of our team members, also prayed about the girl's dilemma. It was the sort of answer described in Isaiah 30:21 where it says, "Your ears shall hear a voice behind you, saying, 'This is the way, walk in it,' whether you turn to the right or whether you turn to the left."

To Samuel, with mechanical skills, laying on his hotel bed and unable to sleep, the Lord's voice sounded more like this: "Cut the axel a little this way.... Make an adjustment on the crossbar that way.... turn the wrench to the right, and turn to the left ... and you'll have it. You'll be able to fix that chair for Claudia."

The following morning Samuel got right to work on the leftover pediatric wheelchair that had seemed so unsuitable and unusable. And he got it fixed just in time, only moments before the determined Peruvian woman with her little disabled daughter came back to the center.

She had prayed. Samuel had prayed. And God miraculously answered.

From India: Out of the Tunnel

Mahesh was a leader in his family, a highly educated man with an impeccable British accent. But then one night he had a fall—off the edge of his home's balcony, badly breaking both of his legs. Although his legs were cast, they never properly healed, and he became a paraplegic.

His disability disgraced his family, and they put him out on the streets.

When we met Mahesh and heard his story, we were stunned. Could it really be? Would a man's own family actually treat him in such a way? But Mahesh only shrugged, telling us that this was the tradition in India. After all, he reminded us, he had lost all his respect. When we first encountered him, he was living inside a tunnel that linked two highways together. His bed was nothing but a filthy bed of rags and threadbare towels, and he had been living there for several years.

Thankfully our team members spotted him as they were driving through town. We were amazed that this man who looked like a beggar was so educated and well-spoken. He was just as amazed that these foreigners would actually stop and talk to an outcast like himself.

Through an interpreter, we were able to share the gospel of Christ with him, and the next day we returned to the tunnel with a wheelchair. We worked hard to custom-fit him, right there in that tunnel on the sidewalk between two highways. Then our team members took him to a health care clinic and connected him with an Indian ministry that works with the disabled.

Mahesh is now being restored to society and to wholeness—yes, because of the clinic and the work of some local churches, but best of all because of Jesus Christ. Yes, that's right: Mahesh became a Christian, and it's made all the difference in his life. God's healing love became more real in that filthy tunnel than in any glorious cathedral. It's what happens when you touch the untouchable in Jesus' name.

From Cameroon: "Where Is My Food?"

Amidou is a Muslim man who was paralyzed as a result of a stroke and had been in that condition for several years. When our team met him, he was badly in need of help.

After we fit this elderly gentleman to his new wheelchair, he listened very intently, especially as we gave the gospel to him, explaining the salvation message using the colored beads of a gospel bracelet. We told him the black bead represented his sin; the red, Christ's blood; the white bead was for forgiveness; and the green bead represented growth, and so on.

As our worker explained the green bead, Amidou suddenly said, "Where is the food for my growth? I am hungry for this food that others are receiving."

We realized that Amidou wasn't talking about physical food, but rather about the Bible that he had seen others receive that same morning. So we wasted no time in giving a French Bible to Amidou and his wife, Adizai. They were absolutely fascinated, and Adizai told us that although she had heard the name of Jesus, she'd never had any details. She was amazed to hear that He was still alive!

It's difficult to describe the joy on this former Muslim couple's faces as they left the distribution center that day. Patting the cover of their new Bible, Amidou said, "Surely we will eat this food. Such a God we have never known before."

From Thailand: A Left-Handed Wheelchair

Last year when we were in Thailand, we were unloading our wheelchairs in Bangkok when we noticed a chair designed for a person with only one arm—the left arm.

If you turned just one wheel on a normal wheelchair you would, of course, go in circles. But this particular wheelchair had a long lever mechanism that could be pumped by a person's left arm in order to propel it forward. When our team members saw that chair, we scratched our heads. It seemed really odd, and we couldn't understand how it made its way into the group of all the other wheelchairs. It was way too specialized. There was no one on our Thailand list who was a paraplegic without use of his or her right arm.

After a busy week of distribution, just as we were about to close the distribution center, a man crawled in off the street. His name was Francis, and he had just heard that we were in town. So he had crawled onto a bus and had traveled from a far distance to find us. When he arrived, he crawled into the distribution center dragging his feet behind him, and using only one arm to do so.

His left arm.

Miraculously, Francis had been able to pull the weight of his body with only his left arm. We learned he had been injured in a work accident several years earlier and never received proper care. But that day we gave him not only good health care, we gave him a wheelchair that fit him perfectly. It was that crazy ultra-specialized chair with the lever mechanism that a person could operate with his left hand.

It was the perfect chair and a perfect fit for Francis.

Who knew?

God knew.

From West Africa: Mal's Testimony

Seventy-five-year-old Mal, a master mechanic who hailed from Minnesota, was one of our most senior team members. Just a year before journeying with our Wheels team to West Africa, Mal had been in a coma, almost dead. But the doctors gave him a medication that had brought him back from the edge and saved his life. Nevertheless, when he emerged from the hospital, it was with both legs amputated below the knee.

Most people would have been crushed by that development, thinking they had lost everything. But Mal was grateful to have his life back, and had promised the Lord that whatever door of ministry He might open up, Mal would step through—legs or no legs.

Six months later when a door opened for Mal to become a member of one of our teams delivering wheelchairs and Bibles to West Africa, he strapped on his prosthetic legs and signed up as a wheelchair mechanic. Mal did a phenomenal job with his screwdriver and hacksaw, fixing all the wheelchairs and fitting them perfectly to the needs of each disabled person.

But here's the real reason God wanted Mal on that trip.

The Africans—especially the older ones—were drop-jawed amazed at this elderly man who was so confidently walking about and helping others *while he was standing on steel legs.* Mal's faith in his sovereign God was a powerful testimony to the many families who came to the wheelchair distribution. He was a living audiovisual aid of John 9:3 (ESV): "that the works of God might be displayed in him."

Many Africans—including a large number of elderly men and women—came to Christ during that wheelchair distribution. The wheelchairs were a dream come true, and they readily accepted the gospel of Jesus Christ. But what had won their hearts was a seventy-five-year-old man with no legs who came across half the earth to help others in need.

From Egypt: Yasser's New Friends

My friend Rebecca Atallah runs a camp for disabled children who live on a garbage dump outside of Cairo, Egypt. It's called the Garbage Village Camp, and sometimes a lot of adults show up at her camp.

Like Yasser.

He's a thirty-year-old Egyptian man whose legs were amputated just a few years ago. Although he's got a wheelchair—something many disabled people throughout the world could only dream about—Yasser struggles with depression over his loss. Concerned about his situation, Rebecca allowed him to stay more than one week at camp.

Gently but persistently, Rebecca challenged Yasser to start working and supporting himself again. At first he wasn't sure what he could do, but later he told Rebecca that he might be able to go into the tin-can recycling business, scavenging for soda cans in the vast garbage dump. The tops of soft drink cans are made of aluminum, and are worth five times as much as the rest of the can. People who live on scavenging the dumps, however, usually don't have access to the special scissors required to cut off the tops of the cans. They have to turn in the whole cans for recycling, and their tiny earnings are worth even less. Lots of children who live on the edge of these mountains of garbage help their families make a livelihood from recycling.

But how could Yasser, a double amputee, compete with the children for cans—or navigate his wheelchair through all those great mounds of trash? It overwhelmed him to think about, and he was almost ready to declare defeat before he even began his venture. That's when Rebecca offered to collect cans for him, if he would do the work of cutting off the tops of all the cans. Yasser was very grateful, and eagerly accepted the offer. With strong and able hands, this was something he could certainly do.

It wasn't long before news of the little arrangement between Rebecca and Yasser spread through the camp. A group of deaf teenagers at the camp were taking an afternoon walk and started talking—actually, *signing*—to each other about Yasser and his hope of starting a small recycling business.

As they were walking and signing, they started noticing all the soda cans strewn alongside the dirt road. *That* gave them an idea. A couple of them ran back and got some plastic bags so they could start collecting these throw-away cans by the side of the path. They brought back three very large bagfuls of cans for Yasser to work on!

When Rebecca saw this, she was overwhelmed. With tears in her eyes, she told me, "Joni, these deaf young people have so much pain in their lives … so much rejection. Here they are, suffering so much, and yet they were moved by the Lord to share in Yasser's plight—and in such a practical way!"

To me, it's such a wonderful illustration of that beautiful verse in Galatians where we are told to bear one another's burdens. Yes, we have our aches and pains. Yes, we have our sorrows and disappointments. I have my quadriplegia and chronic pain, and you have your own set of difficulties and challenges. But always and always, Scripture forces us to keep considering the needs of others, no matter how little you have, or how difficult your experiences.

And I thank those young, deaf Egyptian teens for not focusing on their own afflictions, but rather getting excited about bearing the burden of Yasser—a man with no legs, but with a fresh grip on hope.

TEN

THANK YOU, GOD, FOR THIS WHEELCHAIR

O LORD, you are my God;
I will exalt you and praise your name,
for in perfect faithfulness
you have done marvelous things,
things planned long ago.

—Isaiah 25:1

Her name is Shantamma.

When our Wheels team was in India recently, we met this bright-eyed eighteen-year-old, from a Hindu family living in Ongole.

No one born in the poverty and despair of the teeming slums of this city has an easy life. But many have had it easier than Shantamma. Born with a disability, she has spent her life scooting around on the floor of the family's tiny home, dragging her legs behind her and rarely venturing outside her front door.

The message of good news in Christ, however, has permeated this coastal city of 300,000. Four years previous to our meeting Shantamma, an evangelical pastor from a small church made contact with the family. When he learned of Shantamma's condition, he went back to his little office, picked up his tattered copy of an old *Joni* book out of his meager library, and brought it to the young woman as a gift.

Although a Hindu her whole life, Shantamma read that book cover to cover. With tears running down her cheeks, she made up her mind to trust in Jesus Christ … *just like Joni*. In fact, she read that book eight times, rehearsing over and over how a person could come to salvation through Jesus. And finally, that is what she did. In a big decision that undoubtedly had consequences within her family and her community, Shantamma left the Hindu religion and became a Christian.

Then our team came, bringing wheelchairs and Bibles to Ongole to deliver to needy disabled people. After all those years of crawling and dragging herself from place to place, Shantamma learned to her wonder and delight that she was to receive her own wheelchair. The chair, however, had an excitement for her that went far beyond the gift itself. These were followers of Jesus who were giving those wheelchairs to people! Shantamma was so proud and excited to think that the God she had learned to trust from reading the *Joni* book so many times, that *this* God—*her* own God—was showing her this special kindness and providing an opportunity for her to receive an actual wheelchair fit just for her.

After Shantamma was finally fitted for her chair, however, she was shocked and stunned to learn where the chairs had come from. She burst into tears when she realized that these wheelchairs were sent "by her very own Joni, from so far away."

Since that day, Shantamma has experienced a new level of joy and confidence, and has become more emboldened to share her faith in Christ with friends and neighbors still locked in the Hindu religion. She said to one of our team members, "I am ready to go wherever God leads me in this wheelchair … *just like Joni*."

My friends, this is one of a million reasons why I am grateful God didn't heal me of my paralysis. What if I had been healed at the Kathryn Kuhlman crusade back in the early 1970s? What if God had answered my prayers as a seventeen-year-old, released me from my paralysis, and returned me to a normal life of a woman on her feet?

It might have been well for me, but what about Shantamma?

There would have been no *Joni* book for the pastor to give this young woman with so little hope and so few prospects, and there would have been no Joni and Friends or Wheels for the World to do a wheelchair distribution for impoverished people in Ongole, India.

Would Shantamma have come to Jesus anyway? Would God have gained glory and would the name of Jesus have been held high in those slums through her bright, joyful testimony?

That is a mystery of God's providence, and as someone has said, is "above my pay grade." In C. S. Lewis's children's classic *Prince Caspian*, Lucy asks the great lion Aslan what would have happened if she had made a different choice at a crucial crossroads in her journey through Narnia. Aslan replied to her, "To know what *would* have happened, child? No, nobody is ever told that."

I can't know what would have happened to Shantamma if there had been no quadriplegic girl in America named Joni to inspire her and lead her to faith in the one true God. Perhaps, as Mordecai told Esther, "relief and deliverance" for this girl would have arisen "from another place."

I only know that because I wasn't healed, because God had plans for my life that were wider and higher and deeper and more profound than I could have ever imagined, a teenage girl named Shantamma from the slums of urban India will be with me in heaven. In glorious new bodies that will never tire and never fade, we'll explore the high mountains of that place, and the wide, green meadows, and we will laugh out loud for joy over the goodness and grace of our heavenly Father.

What will those decades of disability mean to me *then?* What will those few years of chronic pain, tears, and frustration add up to *then?*

That's enough right there to cause me to say, "Thank you, God, for this wheelchair."

That's one story. Let me give you just one more.

Every time we go on a trip of any kind, I ask the Lord to show us His favor, to reveal Himself to us here, there, and everywhere along the way.

Not long ago my friends Bev and Francie and I came back to our hotel after I had spoken at a school for the physically disabled. The house-keeper was still cleaning my hotel room, so I went into Bev and Francie's room right next door (we always get connecting rooms so we can easily run back and forth). Anyway, as we were waiting, we happened to notice a little handwritten note on Bev's side table. It was from the housekeeper. She had just cleaned the room and had written these words on a hotel notepad:

> *Dear Joni, I read your book when I first became a Christian in 1980, and the Lord used you to see me through some very tough times.*

Was it the same housekeeper who was now cleaning my room? That's what I wanted to find out, so I wheeled into the adjoining room and asked the young woman who was tucking in the corners of the bedsheets, "Pardon me; did you leave a note for me next door?"

The little housekeeper looked up, eyes wide. Immediately she grabbed a pillow off the bed, buried her face in it, and began to cry. In between sobs, I learned that her name was Rachel, and that she had read my book and then seen the *Joni* movie on Christian television. It had been a wonderful blessing to her, she told me.

"No, Rachel," I replied, "*you* are the blessing to us today, because you are an answer to prayer. We had asked the Lord Jesus to encourage us as we left that school a few minutes ago, to help us sense His favor. And we came back here to this hotel, and He's got you waiting for us. Waiting to deliver a blessing!"

Yes, it's just another little incident from my life—not very dramatic, I suppose. But it is stories like these on which my life hinges. Because of the *Joni* book, and the *Joni* movie that grew out of it, a young woman named Rachel, facing a turning point in her own life in 1980, found courage in Christ to go on. What were those "tough times" she was facing in that dark season of her youth? I don't know, and I may never know.

But I do know that when God chose not to heal me, He was seeing little Rachel in His mind's eye, loving her, and wanting to provide for her and comfort her heart. And He was seeing Shantamma, who was wondering if anyone in the world could ever help her or care for her as she dragged herself around her little house in Ongole. And He was seeing thousands, perhaps millions of others whom I will never meet on this side of heaven, whose lives were somehow touched by the story of a paralyzed girl in her wheelchair.

And thinking of that, I am filled with awe, and say again, "Thank You, God, for this wheelchair."

"Marvelous Things ... Planned Long Ago"

Not long ago I came across these amazing words in the book of Isaiah:

> O LORD, you are my God;
> I will exalt you and praise your name,
> for in perfect faithfulness
> you have done marvelous things,
> things planned long ago. (Isa. 25:1)

In a time of spiritual confusion, national decline, and world turmoil, in a day when storms brooded on the horizon and the sounds of war rumbled in the distance, the prophet Isaiah took time to reflect on God's perfect faithfulness, marvelous deeds, and unfathomable plans.

Lord, he said, *no matter what happens, I claim You as my one-and-only God. You're mine! No matter what anyone else chooses to say or do all around me, I'm going to lift up Your name as high as I can for as long as I live, and place my full confidence in Your plans. Lord, You are the Faithful One. Long ago, You looked forward to this very day, and You have planned all of it—marvelous things! Thank You, God, for this ministry You have given me.*

A difficult ministry? A heartbreaking task sometimes?

To be sure.

From the very beginning, he'd been told that his immediate audience wasn't going to listen to him or heed his words. Their hearts would be calloused; their ears would be dull; their eyes would be closed.[1] He was asked to do some very difficult things, things that would have been humiliating and an assault on his dignity as a gentleman and a man of God.[2]

But in his heart of hearts, Isaiah was thankful. He had told the Lord, "Here am I. Send me!" and didn't look back. God's plan was the best of all possible plans, and therefore the life he had been given—difficult as it may have been—was the best life he could have asked for.

And anyway, he knew what was ahead! Though the saints in the Old Testament didn't have all of the revelation that we do on heaven, Isaiah had been given a bright vision that burned and blossomed and danced in his mind's eye. In the same chapter, just a few verses later, he wrote:

> On this mountain the LORD Almighty will prepare
>   a feast of rich food for all peoples....
> On this mountain he will destroy
>   the shroud that enfolds all peoples,
>   the sheet that covers all nations;
> he will swallow up death forever.
>   The Sovereign LORD will wipe away the tears
>   from all faces;
>   he will remove the disgrace of his people

from all the earth.
The LORD has spoken. (25:6–8)

I will add my voice of praise to his.

Thank You, God, for this life You have given me. Thank You for the many opportunities to serve You, even in my pain. *Thank You, God, for this wheelchair. For it's been granted to me to not only believe on Your Son, but to suffer for His sake. Oh joy!*

> *... For in perfect faithfulness*
> *you have done marvelous things,*
> *things planned long ago.*

As I have stated in the pages of this book, so many have tried to get me to say that my accident forty-three years ago was never part of God's plan. That my paralysis was never His intention. That quadriplegia was never necessary. That chronic pain didn't have to be. That suffering was never part of His plan. That the many tears and groans and struggles and sleepless nights were needless and a waste of my energy and my life.

I know differently.

It was all planned long ago, and God brought it about in His perfect faithfulness. And because He allowed it and permitted it, because He has walked with me through every moment of it, His plan has been marvelous for Joni Eareckson Tada.

And let me add this. I mean these words as much as I have ever meant any words:

I am content.

The Secret of Contentment
"I'm glad in God, far happier than you would ever guess...."

Paul wrote from a lonely prison cell, far from home, and cut off from friends, family, fresh air, and the light of day. He'd been incarcerated for simply being a believer in Jesus Christ—and having the gall to talk about it and teach others about Him. But if his enemies thought that the dungeon would break his spirit, they couldn't have been further from the truth.

"Actually," he went on, "I don't have a sense of needing anything personally. I've learned by now to be quite content whatever my circumstances. I'm just as happy with little as with much, with much as with little. I've found the recipe for being happy whether full or hungry, hands full or hands empty. Whatever I have, wherever I am, I can make it through anything in the One who makes me who I am."[3]

"Glad in God"?

"Far happier than you would ever guess"?

"I've found the recipe for happiness"?

It really doesn't make much logical sense, does it? How could the apostle Paul be content—even joyful—over so little?

It reminds me of meeting Summer last year—a beautiful, young, athletic girl who had been trained as a lifeguard. Not long ago she broke her neck and is now paralyzed and in a wheelchair.

On the day we visited, however, Summer had something exciting to share with me. She wanted to show me how she could move her wrists a little bit and make tiny movements in one or two of her fingers.

"Wow!" I said. "That's *awesome!* How wonderful! You have every reason to hope big that you'll get back more. People who are spinal-cord injured can regain a lot within the first year."

The people standing around us smiled, looking on with curiosity. I'm sure we looked a little odd. Here we were, both in wheelchairs, both severely paralyzed—no use of our legs or feet, limited arm movement, no use of hands—and knowing full well that the bulk of our paralyses are permanent.

And yet …

We were thrilled at the fact that young Summer could move her wrist an eensy-weensy eighth to a quarter of an inch. Really, it was almost imperceptible, but if you looked very carefully, you could see that joint move ever so slightly. By some secret and incomprehensible pathway, a command from Summer's brain was somehow sneaking around or through the massive neural roadblock created by her injury, and there was movement, blessed *movement*, in one of her limbs. And she and I were ecstatic. We laughed and talked as excitedly as if she had just completed her first marathon, graduated from college, or announced her engagement.

"But it was no big deal," you say. "It was just a tiny movement."

Yes, but when you're paralyzed, you measure happiness in quarter-inch increments. A quarter-inch of good news, received from the Lord with a grateful heart, can bring as much joy as half a mile of good news to an indifferent or cynical heart.

As we celebrated together, it was as though the dreadful reality that 90-plus percent of her body was paralyzed didn't really matter in those moments … and didn't even figure into the equation.

And do you know what? It truly didn't.

Summer had an equation for contentment, and her paralysis simply didn't show up in the calculation.

Sometimes you have to look at the glass half-full rather than half-empty. More than that, even when there's only a few drops in the bottom of the glass, you have to think, "There's *something* in there. Isn't that wonderful? It could be empty, but no, there's something to rejoice about!"

And so you do, as joyously and with as full a heart as the Lord enables you.

Summer has every reason to hope that she'll get back yet a little more movement in her hands. Maybe she'll graduate to half an inch, or even one-inch movements. If she does, we'll go ballistic. The party will be on. *But even if she doesn't*, I do believe this young woman will still be content. Contentment is realizing that God has already given her everything she needs for her present happiness. It is the wise person who doesn't grieve for the things he *doesn't* have, but rejoices over the things he *does* have.

Have you prayed for healing and God has said "wait" or "no"? Will you be content with Him, and Him alone, even if your most fervent prayers are placed on hold?

Summer has learned (and is learning) the lesson that Fanny Crosby, the blind hymn writer of an earlier generation, once observed. She said, "O what a happy soul am I! Although I cannot see, I am resolved that in this world contented I will be; how many blessings I enjoy that other people don't! To weep and sigh because I'm blind, I cannot, and I won't."

Glass half-full people are called optimists, and it truly is the best and happiest way for anyone to live. But we who put our faith in Jesus Christ have something beyond mere optimism, positive thinking, or rose-colored lenses. We have a hope that not only fills our glass halfway, it *overflows* it. Romans 15:13 says, "May the God of hope fill you with all joy and peace as you trust in him, so that you may overflow with hope by the power of the Holy Spirit."

If we have Him, how much else do we really need?

A tiny movement of my friend Summer's wrist filled her with gladness. Strangely enough, that's the way it is when you have very little—when life gets stripped down to the basics.

I had a friend (who can now afford a number of luxuries) tell me that one of the happiest summers of his life was when he was a single young man, freshly graduated from Bible college, working for minimum wage in a bookstore, and living in an upstairs room of an old college dorm house. It was a time of life, he said, when he could fit *all* of his worldly belongings (except a bicycle) into his Volkswagen. He didn't know what was ahead; he had only enough money for room and board (and little else). He met with several guys a couple times a week for one of the most exciting Bible studies he had ever experienced, and in his spare hours, he explored the nearby summer countryside on his bicycle.

It was definitely a transitional phase of life for him, and he wouldn't have wanted to stay in that place forever. But looking back now, he can see it for what it was: a peaceful, joyful interval of life during which he had few responsibilities, fewer possessions, and plenty of time to seek a closer relationship with God.

"I'm just as happy with little as with much, with much as with little. I've found the recipe for being happy whether full or hungry, hands full or hands empty. Whatever I have, wherever I am, I can make it through anything in the One who makes me who I am."[4]

I have another young friend whose life situation is even more restricted and limited than Summer's. Another beautiful, athletic girl—just thirteen years old—and with a great singing voice, Cathe was running down her street trying to make it to school before the late bell rang when she was struck by a fast-moving car. She, too, was totally paralyzed by the accident … but much more so than Summer or I.

Summer can move some fingers and bend her wrist, and I can fling my arms around using my shoulder muscles. But Cathe sits absolutely rigid and must use a ventilator to be able to breathe. She maneuvers her wheelchair by means of pressing her tongue against a special retainer in her mouth.

The last time I saw her, ten years had passed since her accident, and she was a young woman of twenty-three. When I met her, she was poised, personable, and even though she can't speak normally, *she shares a radiant testimony of how Christ has met every need of her life.*

Listen to a few lines from a longer poem she wrote not long ago— timed to the spaces between the breathing of her ventilator.

> Now when people see me
> in my wheelchair bound,

no one knows (though I am still)
the joy that I have found.

My arms they will not move again,
my legs they do not walk,
without my special speaking valve,
I cannot even talk.

These simple facts mean nothing,
these things that you can see,
it's the unseen changes made inside,
by Him who lives in me.

No person knows contentment
such as He has given me,
unless they gave their heart to Him,
then waited patiently,
for Him to do the shaping part,
the way He did for me.

All I Need, I Already Have

Can you sign your name under that statement?

Does that express your heart?

Does it express mine?

I've had to ask that question numerous times—and more so since pain has set ever more severe restrictions on my freedom and abilities.

What do I have?

Unlike my young friend Cathe, I still have a voice. I can speak, I can sing hymns of praise, and I can even talk over the radio to a nationwide audience. Unlike many disabled people I have met around the world, I have a wheelchair. I also have a husband who loves me, friends who care about me, and coworkers who labor at my side in common purpose. Not everyone has been blessed with such truly wondrous gifts as these, but I have.

And according to the Lord, that's all I need. For if there were anything more that I needed, He would have given it to me.

Am I using what I have?

Well, I will admit it's been more difficult lately. It's more difficult to travel, write, paint, and record those radio programs I mentioned. I'm more limited in my activities, but I still show up for work, offering what I have to the Lord for His use, and asking for His help. And I know that I will have that help, because He never gives a task without supplying the need. His command never comes without empowerment.

Am I prepared to lose what I have?

Ah, this is the litmus test of contentment. This one scares me a little. Despite Job's agony, he cried out, "Though he slay me, yet will I hope in him"![5] He was prepared to believe, even to the point of death. To be honest, it frightens me to think about the future sometimes. What if my pain never goes away—or gets even worse? What if my paralysis becomes even more profound, and I lose the few abilities I now possess? Well, deep down I know the answer: My calling isn't only to abandon my future wants, but to trust in God and hand over what I already possess.

Am I ready to receive what I don't have?

What would that be? What might it look like? I have no idea. More responsibility? More open doors? More suffering for His name's sake? I can assure you, my friends, that I'm not looking to "enlarge my borders" like Jabez, and expand my spiritual territory. I'd just be happy if God would simply make my heart larger to receive more of His peace and joy.

How long has it been since you've done a thoughtful inventory of your possessions? The secret of contentment is wrapped up in simple gratitude for what God has already provided you.[6]

Sometimes when the day (or night!) seems long, and life in the wheelchair seems like a heavy weight to bear, I remind myself that my Lord Jesus Himself was handicapped.

Jesus Himself Chose to Be Handicapped

Does that concept startle you just a little?

You know me: I'm always looking to see what God's Word has to say about physical limitations. And when you study the life of Jesus, you have to stop and consider that although our Savior did not have a physical disability per se, He *did* handicap Himself when He came to earth.

Boy, did He ever.

How can I say that for sure? Well, the dictionary defines "handicap" as any difficulty that is imposed on a superior person so as to hamper or disadvantage him, making that person more equal with others.

Certainly, if we use that definition, then Jesus was handicapped.

Think of it!

On one hand, the fullness of God dwelt in Christ, yet on the other hand He "made Himself nothing." He emptied Himself, taking the very nature of a servant. Talk about handicaps! Can you imagine a greater one? To be *God* on one hand, and yet to make Himself nothing! That is one severe limitation which, you would think, would have hampered our Lord or put Him at a disadvantage.

Jesus, the Master Architect of the entire universe, designed suns and stars, galaxies and planets. When He handicapped Himself, He made Himself a carpenter on earth, limiting Himself to designing common wooden chairs, stools, tables, and yokes for necks of oxen.

Jesus was also the one who spoke the Word, creating everything around us. But this same Jesus who spoke time and space into being handicapped Himself on earth, choosing instead to speak to prostitutes, lepers, and sinners.

Jesus, the one who since Satan's fall had despised pain and suffering as one of the awful results of man's sin, handicapped Himself on earth when His back ached and His muscles cramped and when He sweat real sweat and cried real tears and bled real blood.

When I think of all this, it strikes me that these limitations didn't just "happen" to Jesus in the same way that circumstances "happen" to you and me. The amazing thing is that Christ *chose* to be handicapped. I can't think of too many people who would actually choose to be disabled. Believe me, I know I wouldn't! There is nothing easy, nothing fun, nothing casual about dealing with a disability. From the very get-go, it's *hard*.

But Jesus chose to handicap Himself so that you and I might share eternity with Him in bodies that will never stoop, limp, falter, or fail. Jesus chose to experience pain and suffering beyond our imagination in order that you and I would one day walk the streets of heaven whole, happy, and pain free. Jesus chose to die—though that was a daunting task in itself. As C. S. Lewis wrote, Jesus "was so full of life that when He wished to die He had to 'borrow death from others.'"

But borrow it He did, taking it unto Himself, yielding up His life, so that you and I might pass through death's shadow and live forever.

Yes, while I'm alive here on earth, I am called to endure a handicap. But how could I be other than grateful and content? I'm in the best company of all.

One Last Thought: Kneel

Sometimes I will open up the old Book of Common Prayer from the Reformed Episcopal Church I grew up in. At this writing, I was reminded that it will be Epiphany Sunday this weekend. And from the Psalter reading of that day:

*They shall fear thee, as long as the sun and moon
endureth, from one generation to another.*

*He shall come down like the rain upon the mown
grass, even as the drops that water the earth.*

*In his time shall the righteousness flourish; yea, and
abundance of peace, so long as the moon endureth.*

*His dominion shall be also from the River unto the
world's end.*

It makes me want to … *kneel.*

In our little Maryland church, people preached the gospel, read from
the liturgy, sang hymns from the heart, and they kneeled in prayer before
the Lord. Worship was a serious thing, and I learned as a child what it
meant to bend the knee before the Lord.

It's not that I want to make a big thing about kneeling in prayer, per
se. It's just that … I wish I could do it. Being paralyzed in a wheelchair, it's
impossible to literally bend my knees and bow in prayer.

I remember a banquet at a big conference I attended not long ago. I
was sitting along with everyone else in a *huge* ballroom. At the close of the
message, the speaker asked everyone to do something unusual: He asked
us to push our chairs away from the tables and, if we felt comfortable in
doing so, get out of our chairs and kneel on the carpeted floor, together,
in prayer.

Well, I sat there in my wheelchair and watched as everyone else in
the room, maybe five hundred or six hundred people, got out of their
chairs and down on their knees for a brief time of worship. With everyone
kneeling in that great banquet hall, I'm afraid I stood out as the only one
remaining seated.

Looking around the room, I couldn't stop the tears.

Oh, I wasn't crying out of self-pity or because I felt strange or different that I was the only one sitting. My eyes were wet because it was so *beautiful* to see everyone kneeling in prayer. (Maybe I am making a big deal about kneeling!) It made me think of the day when I, too, will be able to get out of this wheelchair on new, resurrected legs.

I can't wait for that day, because when I get my glorified body, the first thing I'm going to do with my new made-for-eternity legs is to fall down on grateful, glorified knees. I will once again have the chance to say with Psalm 95:6: "Come let us bow down in worship, let us kneel before the LORD our Maker."

If you've read any of my previous books, you will know how I have dreamed of the day when I can run, leap, walk, jump, and dance. It will be my privilege: a new body that can move will be my blessing for a job well done on earth. But I think that kneeling very still on bended knees will be my sacrifice of praise. To *not* move when I will at last be able to move will be one last chance to show the Lord how thankful I really am.

So I will kneel …

> … on the bright green turf of heaven's rolling meadows.

> … on an avenue of gold, smooth as glass, clear as an artesian spring, cool as an April breeze, and shot through with fire.

> … with saints from all ages, former kings and queens, apostles and martyrs, farmer's wives and soldiers, and wonderful people through all the years who loved Jesus more than life.

… with mighty angelic beings who knew how to
kneel before they knew how to walk—or fly.

It's been a long time since I've actually kneeled in prayer. Those long-ago days at that little Reformed Episcopal Church seem so far away, softened and made more beautiful in the golden haze of memory.

But the day is drawing near, isn't it? It's drawing so close to the time when I, and so many others who cannot walk, will be able to kneel. I know it. I can feel it. Heaven is just around the corner.

If you sense His coming is soon, would you please do me a favor? Do what so many of us who are paralyzed or too lame or too old or disabled can't do. Would you open your Bible to Psalm 95:6, read it aloud, and then do what it says?

I can't kneel, but if you can, do.

Kneel before the Lord God, your Maker and mine. And while you're down there, if you feel so inclined, thank Him for being so good to a paralyzed woman named Joni.

EPILOGUE

Months have passed since I penned my final word on the previous page, and I cannot let you close this book without an update: I'm holding my breath, hoping I'm not jumping the gun when I say that I'm now enjoying many more good days than bad.

Maybe it's because I'm sitting differently in my wheelchair ... or wearing my corset higher ... or maybe looser. Could it be a change in diet? Drinking more fluids? I breathe more deeply and certainly stretch more often. Or perhaps it's because I'm no longer on that heavy-duty pain medication—you know, the one that has side effects worse than the remedy?

Whatever the reason, I'm waking each morning, blessing God for another day ... and closing my eyes at night, grateful that I still have a role to play in Christ's kingdom. I've resumed a somewhat normal travel schedule, and even have strength enough to stay sitting up all day.

I have a feeling it's because of your prayers—every day my soul seems to vibrate with the repercussions of people's prayers. I trust that the Lord will enable me to keep moving forward in this wheelchair, and if you'd like to track alongside, I invite you to visit "Joni's Corner" at JoniAndFriends.org. There you will find the latest updates as well as a bounty of praise reports to our great and awesome God. And as far as moving into the future? For the remainder of the journey, I hold fast to a courageous and invigorating verse in Acts 20:24, and I invite you to do the same.

I consider my life worth nothing to me, if only I may finish the race
and complete the task the Lord Jesus has given me—
the task of testifying to the gospel of God's grace.

NOTES

Chapter 1

[1] "He Who Began a Good Work in You," performed by Steve Green, *Find Us Faithful*, 1988.

Chapter 2

[1] Dora Greenwell, "I Am Not Skilled to Understand," *Songs of Salvation*, 1873.

[2] Luke 18:1.

[3] Henry Frost, *Miraculous Healing: Why does God heal some and not others?* (Grand Rapids, MI: Revell, 1939; Hagerstown, MD: Christian Heritage, 2000), 36. Citations are to the Christian Heritage edition. This and all subsequent excerpts are taken from *Miraculous Healing: Why does God heal some and not others?* by Henry Frost, published by Christian Focus Publications, Fearn, Ross-shine, Scotland (www. ChristianFocus.com).

[4] New King James Version.

[5] 1 Timothy 5:23.

[6] Acts 12:2.

[7] Revelation 1:9.

[8] Acts 7:59–60.

[9] 2 Timothy 4:20.

[10] Acts 23:11.

[11] Philippians 4:12.

[12] Frost, 37.

[13] Ibid., 37–39.

Chapter 3

[1] Adapted from my foreword to *Miraculous Healing: Why does God heal some and not others?* (Fearn, Ross-shine, Scotland: Christian Focus Publications, 2000).

[2] John 6:68–69 NLT.

[3] The Living Bible.

[4] Frost, 11.

[5] Ibid., 12.

[6] Ibid., 108.

[7] Psalm 103:13–14.

[8] Adapted from Joni Eareckson Tada, *Pearls of Great Price* (Grand Rapids, MI: Zondervan, 2006), August 28 reading.

[9] Richard Mayhue, *Divine Healing Today* (Chicago: Moody Press, 1983), 52–53.

[10] Andrew Wommack, "God Wants You Well," http://www.awmi.net/extra/article/wants_well (accessed February 24, 2010).

[11] Frost, 109–110.

[12] Ibid., 70.

[13] John 21:22.

[14] Frost, 108–109.

[15] Ibid., 116.

[16] Ibid., 69.

[17] Ibid., 13.

[18] Matthew 8:2–3.

[19] Joni Eareckson Tada and Steve Estes, *A Step Further* (Grand Rapids: Zondervan, 1978), 16.

[20] Frost, 106–107.

Chapter 4

[1] Isaiah 40:13.

[2] Edythe Draper, *Draper's Book of Quotations for the Christian World* (Weahton, IL: Tyndale House, 1992), 198.

[3] Jeremiah 2:13.

[4] John Bunyan, *The Acceptable Sacrifice: The Excellency of a Broken Heart in The Works of John Bunyan,* Volume 1 (Shippensburg, PA: Destiny Image Publishers, 2001), 720.

Chapter 5

[1] Psalm 13:2.

[2] Hebrews 4:15 MSG.

[3] Jeremiah 37:20.

[4] 2 Corinthians 12:9 MSG.

[5] Psalm 89:15–17

[6] Author's translation.

Chapter 6

[1] *International Standard Bible Encyclopedia, Electronic Database* (Seattle: Biblesoft, Inc., 1996, 2003), s.v. "glory."

[2] The New Testament in Modern English

[3] 1 Peter 5:6.

[4] Romans 7:24–25; 8:1.

[5] Romans 8:38–39.

Chapter 7

[1] Isaiah 7:9.

[2] Hosea 6:3 ESV.

[3] Romans 15:13 MSG.

[4] "Oh Happy Day That Fixed My Choice," Philip Doddridge, 1755.

Chapter 8

[1] Psalms 22:19; 31:2; 38:22; 40:13; 69:17–18; 70:1; 70:5; 71:12; 79:8; 102:2; 141:1; 143:7.

Chapter 9

[1] Romans 8:18 PH

[2] Hebrews 12:11.

Chapter 10

[1] Isaiah 6:9–10.

[2] Isaiah 20:1–4.

[3] Philippians 4:10, 11–13 MSG.

[4] Philippians 4:10, 11–13 MSG.

[5] Job 13:15.

[6] Adapted from Tada, *Pearls of Great Price,* October 16 reading.

RESOURCES

For a complete list of other books written by Joni Eareckson Tada or for more information about her greeting cards, which she paints by mouth, contact the website of the Joni and Friends International Disability Center at:

www.joniandfriends.org

Or you can write Joni at:

Joni and Friends International Disability Center

P.O. Box 3333

Agoura Hills, CA 91376 USA

818-707-5664

The mission of Joni and Friends is to communicate the gospel and equip Christ-honoring churches worldwide to evangelize and disciple people affected by disability. Premiere programs include Wheels for the World, Family Retreats, the Joni and Friends television series, and a radio outreach aired on over one thousand outlets across America. The Christian Institute on Disability at Joni and Friends partners with Christian universities and seminaries around the world to develop courses of study in disability ministry. Through a network of volunteers and JAF field teams,

Joni and Friends is committed to accelerating Christian ministry into the disability community around the world. If you would like to learn how you can partner in this effort, write Joni and Friends today.